The Ark of the Covenant
Investigating the Ten Leading Claims

Including Pharaoh Shishak's Siege of Solomon's Temple, Ethiopia's Ark, the Garden Tomb Legend, Jerusalem's Secret Temple Chamber, the Copper Scroll & Knights Templar, Parker's 1911 Dig, the Lemba Jews, Mount Sinai / Nebo, and Tutankhamun's Golden Ark

Paul Backholer

The Ark of the Covenant
Investigating the Ten Leading Claims

Copyright © Paul Backholer 2018 - ByFaith Media
www.ByFaith.org - All Rights Reserved

Photographs Copyright © Mathew Backholer
Illustrations Copyright © Paul Backholer

Scripture quotations are taken from the Holy Bible. The New King James Version (NKJV). Published by Thomas Nelson, Inc. Copyright © 1982 by Thomas Nelson, Inc. Used by permission. All rights reserved.

New International Version®. NIV®. Copyright © 1973, 1978, 1984, by International Bible Society. Used by permission of Zondervan. All rights reserved.

Due to the use of American and British terminology, Anglophone spelling and grammar variations are in use.

All rights reserved. No part of this publication may be reproduced, stored in a retrieval system, or transmitted in any form or by any means – electronically, mechanically, photocopying, recording, or any other (except for brief quotations in printed or official website reviews with full accreditation) without the prior permission of the Publisher, ByFaith Media, Paul Backholer, **www.ByFaith.org**. Uploading or downloading of this work from the internet, or any other device (in whole or in part) is illegal, as is unauthorised translations. For requests for Translation Rights, please contact ByFaith Media.

UK ISBN 978-1-78822-001-9

British Library Cataloguing In Publication Data.
A Record of this Publication is available in the British Library.

Published by ByFaith Media.
Copyright © 2018.

Contents

Page		Chapter
4.	Mount Sinai	1.
8.	The Bible, Faith and Archaeology	2.
10.	What was the Ark of the Covenant?	3.
12.	The Burning Bush	4.
14.	The City under the Sea	5.
16.	Tutankhamun's Gold	6.
18.	The Antiquities of the Second Temple	7.
20.	Pharaoh Shishak's Invasion of Judah	8.
22.	The Silver of Solomon's Temple	9.
26.	The Jews in Egyptian Records	10.
28.	The Trail of Jerusalem's Wealth	11.
30.	A Lost Jewish Temple	12.
32.	Pharaoh Hatshepsut's Mission to Africa	13.
34.	Egypt, Sudan and Ethiopia	14.
36.	The Jews of Ethiopia	15.
38.	Underground Rock Churches	16.
44.	A Lost African Civilisation	17.
46.	The Queen of Sheba's Palace?	18.
48.	The Home of the Ethiopian Ark	19.
52.	Last Hope Monastery	20.
54.	Seeing Ethiopia's Ark	21.
60.	Legends of the Ark	22.
62.	The Knights Templar	23.
64.	Parker's Dome of the Rock Excavation	24.
66.	Mount Nebo and Jeremiah	25.
68.	The Garden Tomb Controversy	26.
71.	The Lemba Jews of South Africa	27.
72.	The Copper Scroll Treasure Hunt	28.
74.	Jerusalem's Secret Temple Chamber	29.
76.	St. John's Revelation of the Heavenly Ark	30.
78.	ByFaith - Quest for the Ark of the Covenant	
79.	ByFaith Media Books	

Mount Sinai

"Look now toward heaven and count the stars if you are able to number them...so shall your descendants be" Genesis 15:5.

The sun was setting on the Sinai Peninsula and my brother Mathew and I were on the summit of the traditional site of Mount Sinai. We were the last to ascend that day, as a snowstorm had made people question the safety of such a venture in bad weather. We too had wondered if it was wise to walk on the snow covered steps to the top, with the expectation of finding ice on the way down. If we fell in the twilight there would be no rescue until morning. But this was a once in a lifetime opportunity, so we balanced the risk with the years of disappointment for regressing and then the choice was obvious.

With the light fading swiftly, we knew we had to descend rapidly without slipping on the ice. Two hours later, with a prayer of thanks we arrived at the base. Suddenly Mathew looked at me and said, "Paul, look up!" During the descent our eyes had been pinned to the ground, making sure we did not lose our footing and fall in the dark, and therefore we had missed the heavens above. As I looked up to the sky, I was amazed. Never before had I seen such a sight. Due to light pollution, the stars which I had seen from Britain seemed small, delicate and distant. However, in this desert I saw many thousands of gleaming balls of light overwhelming the sky. The darkness was squeezed out of the sky, with numerous stars three times the size I had ever seen before, circled by thousands of smaller glows of light. For the first time, I began to understand the challenge and promise to Abraham, "Count the stars, if you are able to number them…so shall your descendants be." As I gazed upward, I knew I could not count them. They were in my mind without number - an extravagant witness of the shining and shimmering promise to the Father of the Jews. Hundreds of years later, the Bible confirms that this promise was being fulfilled as a substantial force of Hebrew slaves escaped out of Egypt, to converge at Mount Sinai. It was during this solemn assembly that Moses had a vision from God to build the Ark of the Covenant. The Ark became the most sacred object to the ancient people of Israel and was placed inside Solomon's Temple (artist's impression below). After Solomon's death the Kingdom was divided into Israel and Judah; this demarcation weakened the people of the Bible, and made them easy pickings for the predatory nations and empires that invaded Jerusalem, and stole their wealth. It was in this context that the Ark of the Covenant was lost to history.

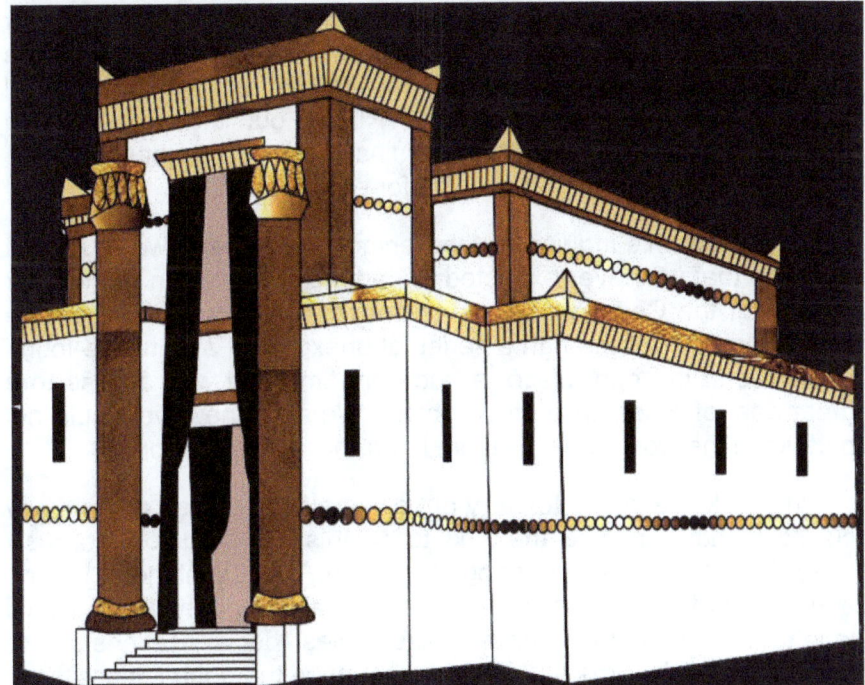

The Ark of the Covenant bequeaths us with many of the greatest unanswered questions of the Bible. What did the Ark look like? Where did it go? When did it disappear and does it still exist today?

The Bible's Ark has captured the imagination like no other sacred object of antiquity, and over many centuries adventurers have searched and presented theories concerning the lost Ark. Many of these conclusions teach us more about the power of the human imagination, rather than the history of the Ark itself. Archaeologists and explorers have spent millions chasing shadows, rumours and interpretations of ancient texts in their search for the Ark, and they all are transfixed by one tantalising question - How could something so distinguished and powerful vanish from history?

In this investigation into the mystery of the lost Ark of the Covenant we have discovered that some have projected their own desires and creative dreams into their hunt for answers, seeing things that no-one else has seen and claiming to have found secret chambers, lost routes and artefacts that never materialise. The 'evidence' is always just around the next corner, yet always out of sight. Many have followed legends, maps and speculative fantasies with the hope of solving the oldest question about the world's most famous treasure.

With these warnings in mind, we wanted to be assured that our quest would not be one into our own imagination, but founded on the cornerstone of rigorous analyse, trusted scholarship, logical research and verifiable artefacts. Ruling out theories, refuting legends and using research to eliminate claims has been just as important in this pursuit, as probing for empirical data.

As we begin this inquiry into the enigma of the Ark, we must first concede that we never expected to partake in a mission to 'hunt for the Ark of the Covenant.' This was never a secret hope, a private plan or dream, yet through a series of unexpected events, we found ourselves in the right place, at the right time and with access to a great deal of research on the subject. We also knew we would not partake in the work of excavation, but rather of exploration.

In this task, we intend to carry out a veracious autopsy of the many claims to have located the Ark; to do this we need to vigorously check and challenge every cognitive intent, idea, sentiment, theory, and alleged find. Before us was a remarkable journey which would lead to ancient Egyptian tombs, desert cities, lost civilisations and to a cornucopia of claims and legends that need thorough assessing.

The Bible, Faith and Archaeology
'That we should no longer be children, tossed to and fro and carried about with every wind of doctrine' Ephesians 4:14.

There are over two billion Christians, who according to orthodox teaching believe that the Bible is God's revelation to man. These believers represent the largest majority of any religious group or worldview on earth. No other faith has played such an enormous role in shaping the world as Christianity has and for this reason the Bible is the most vigorously contested book in world history.

The debate into the history of the Bible's text has split experts and archaeologists into three camps; those who trust in the reliability of Scripture, those who believe there is an element of truth and those who are convinced that most, if not all is fiction. The great multitudes of people therefore find themselves like a sail boat in the ocean, blown about by every wind and wave of opinion. For this reason, people receive contradictory messages concerning the stories of the Bible and archaeological evidence. For example, if an individual watches an expert on TV suggesting that a certain event in the Bible never took place, doubt is formed. But then, the same person goes on to read another study by an expert which comes to the opposite conclusion. Confusion is the outcome - who is telling the truth? Within this context, there appears to be two ways of approaching the Bible and archaeology. The first is to present an opinion about the veracity of the biblical text based on what has not been found; the second is to present an opinion based on what has been found. The secular media tend to take the first approach, whilst many Christians are oblivious to the biblical finds which have been made.

Before we begin our investigation into the location of the lost Ark of the Covenant we have to ask one question: Has any evidence been found for the Ark's existence? Unfortunately for archaeologists there is no easy answer to this question. The proposed site of Solomon's Temple in Jerusalem, where the Ark resided, is currently occupied by the Dome of the Rock Shrine and archaeological exploration is forbidden on the grounds of political and religious claims. A great deal of construction work has been carried out on the Temple Mount and there have been reports from conscientious Arabs that ancient Hebrew texts have been found and destroyed. These accounts are difficult to substantiate, for no-one wants to be identified as a traitor to the Arabs. Nevertheless, the Temple Mount Salvage Operation is sifting through the 'rubbish' that was dug up and dumped by the authorities working on the Temple Mount, and they have recovered artefacts dating back to the First Temple period and arrow heads from the time of the Babylonian invasion of Judah! We now have archaeological evidence that proves the Babylonians were fighting on the Temple Mount as the Bible describes and it was at this time that the Ark was lost. Anyhow, as excavations are not permitted on the Temple Mount to search for Solomon's Temple, or the resting place of the Ark, we can only begin our search by considering just two artefacts, out of many, which collaborates biblical history.

In my last book *The Exodus Evidence*, we examined the case for the Hebrew exodus out of Egypt. In this process we came to the Temple of Pharaoh Merneptah, where we saw the Merneptah Stela, a 3,200 year old stone containing the first record of Israel outside of  the Bible! This stela proves beyond all contradiction, that several hundred years before the Bible indicates that Solomon built a Temple in Jerusalem, an ancient people called Israel were living in the land of Canaan. The second artefact that we must consider is the Tel Dan Stele, dating roughly to 850 years before Christ. This Aramaic inscription includes 'Israel' and the 'House of David.' This is the first reference to the Kingdom of David outside of the Bible, approximately 120 years after his death. This stone indicates that the surrounding kingdoms recognised Israel as a nation and acknowledged that David was the founder of a dynasty of rulers. We do not have any evidence that Israel had the Ark of the Covenant in their possession, but with 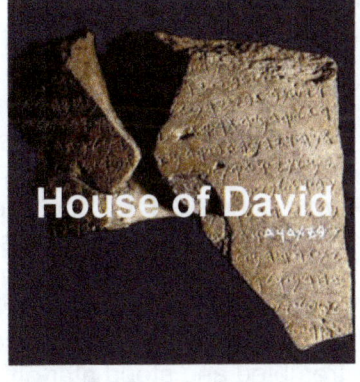 these inscriptions confirming the biblical account, we do not need to take a great leap of faith to believe that these people did indeed produce and revere a golden chest, which contained their law.

What was the Ark of the Covenant?
"Make an Ark of acacia wood...overlay it with pure gold, inside and out" Exodus 25:10-12.

According to the Bible, it was in the region of the Sinai Peninsula that the Ark of the Covenant was conceived and made. Somewhere in this vast desert, the holiest object in world history was born.

But what did the Ark look like? From the Bible's book of Exodus, we learn that God instructed Moses at Mount Sinai to build a sacred wooden container to hold the two tablets of the covenant made between God and His people. This wooden chest, called the Ark of the Covenant was made out of acacia wood, and was overlaid inside and out with gold. It was almost four feet long and just over two feet wide and high, with a mercy seat and two cherubim on top. We learn from Exodus 37:1 that Moses commissioned a skilled man named Bezalel to make the Ark within specific guidelines.

The Ark of the Covenant held the sacred laws of God and it was symbolic of God's relationship with His people. To understand the importance of the Ark to ancient Israel, we must first be aware that it was conceived on the mountain of the Lord during a powerful revelation of God's holiness, judgment, glory and might. 'Now Mount Sinai was completely in smoke, because the Lord had descended upon it in fire...and the whole mountain quaked greatly...Now all the people witnessed the thunderings, the lightning flashes...and they trembled and stood afar off' Exodus 19:18, 20:18.

When God revealed Himself to Israel, His potent manifestation made the people tremble in holy fear. The first revelation of God to Israel was overwhelming. The message to His chosen nation was distinct. God is Almighty, He is holy and sinful mankind dare not come near Him, Exodus 19:21. The design for the Ark of the Covenant was given at this time, and as a consequence the Ark was a practical demonstration of the separation between God and man. How could a holy God abide with the sinful people of Israel?

On the sacred mountain, orders were also given for the design of the Tabernacle, the forerunner to Solomon's Temple. This large tent was made for religious ceremonies and was separated into special areas, with the Holy of Holies closed off to almost everyone. It was in this hallowed section of the Holiest of All that the Ark was to rest. "Then you shall bring the Ark of the Testimony in there, behind the veil. The veil shall be a divider for you, between the holy place and the Most Holy" Exodus 26:33.

The New Testament explains that God used the design of the Tabernacle to unveil the mystery of His plan for mankind's redemption. 'Into the second part (of the Tabernacle) the high priest went alone once a year, not without blood, which he offered for himself and for the people's sins...The Holy Spirit indicating this, that the way into the Holiest of All (heaven) was not yet manifest while the first Tabernacle was still standing' Hebrews 9:7-8.

Kept inside the Ark were the two tablets of the Testimony of God's covenant with Israel, the golden pot containing the manna which the Israelites ate in the wilderness and Aaron's rod, Hebrews 9:4. On the outside of the Ark, two poles made out of acacia wood were held in place by golden rings and only the Levites were allowed to carry the Ark in the prescribed manner. Those who ignored the sacred precepts for carrying it were struck dead, 2 Samuel 6:6-7. Hollywood and some authors have indicated that the Ark had some mystical power, but the Bible verifies that when Israel put her faith in the Ark, rather than the Lord, they forfeited God's protection and were defeated by their enemies, 1 Samuel 4:5-10. Yet, ancient Israel did take the Ark with them into battle and it symbolised God's presence among them, fighting on their behalf, Joshua 6:6-8. When the Ark was carried it had to be covered with a veil, badger skins and a blue cloth. The people were not to see the Ark, Numbers 4:5-6.

Finally, the Ark was designed by God to be the place where He spoke with the leaders of His people. "I will speak with you from above the mercy seat, from between the two cherubim which are on the Ark of the Testimony" Exodus 25:22.

The Burning Bush

'The Angel of the Lord appeared to him in a flame of fire from the midst of a bush' Exodus 3:2.

In our last exodus investigation, we learnt that no-one has proved conclusively where Mount Sinai is located. Yet we did confirm that it is not situated in the currently favoured location of Saudi Arabia. When Paul wrote that Mount Sinai is in Arabia, he was using the Roman understanding of this expression, which included the Sinai Peninsula, Galatians 4:25. He was not using a twenty-first century map and pointing out Saudi Arabia. The text in Exodus 18 leaves no doubt that the mountain of God is not in Saudi Arabia. Moses' father-in-law left his home in Midian (Saudi Arabia) and met Moses at Mount Sinai, Exodus 18:1-6, 27. Later, 'Moses let his father-in-law depart (from Mount Sinai) and he went his way to his own land' (Saudi Arabia). In Numbers 10:29-33, Moses' father-in-law confirms again that Mount Sinai is not in Midian by stating on this second occasion at the mountain, "I will depart to my own land."

With this in mind, we visited the traditional site of Mount Sinai to aid our understanding of the terrain where the Ark of the Covenant was crafted into existence, Exodus 36-40. When we entered Saint Katherine's Monastery, we rapidly came to appreciate that the thin line between legend and historical fact can be blurred with ease.

The priests stated without any reservation, that the bush which was draping down into the courtyard was indeed the same burning bush that Moses had seen! This monastery has a very prestigious heritage, therefore it was a shame to overstep the mark into fiction. However, the experience at the real burning bush transformed Moses' life from a shepherd living a quiet life, to a spiritual leader that led Israel out of Egypt, to the desert where the Ark was made.

This wonderful religious residence at the base of the traditional site of Mount Sinai is one of the oldest Christian monasteries in the world. It is the home of ancient copies of the Scriptures, priceless art and a Christian witness that has lasted for over one and a half millennia. We were hoping to find some inspiration for our quest for the Ark of the Covenant, but there were no leads, so our mission took us onward through the Sinai Peninsula and towards Alexandria. Would we find any clues in that renowned ancient city?

The City under the Sea
'A certain Jew named Apollos, born at Alexandria ...and mighty in the Scriptures' Acts 18:24.

After a lengthy drive we arrived in Alexandria, the city that launched a thousand legends. Cleopatra's palace once stood here; she was the last pharaoh of Egypt and when she died, ancient Egypt was soon buried with her. Thousands of years of history came crashing to the ground with her last breath, as Egypt became just another province in the Roman Empire. Alexander the Great founded this city and it boasted an ancient wonder. The lighthouse of Alexandria was one of the seven wonders of the ancient world and it was the first sight ships would see as they came close to port. When ships docked they were searched for books which were copied for the greatest library of the ancient world. The old library, whose precise location is unknown, would have stored an ancient copy of the Torah. In Alexandria, there was a large Jewish community and it was in this city that the Hebrew Bible was translated into Greek. In consequence could we learn anything about the Ark here? We spent some time in the new library, with no success. After the library, we examined the ancient sites and artefacts of Alexandria. We found items from the Egyptian, Greek and Roman periods, and biblical manuscripts from the early Christian era, but no clues to the Ark.

Little remains of ancient Alexandria, but her history is extraordinary; in the early Christian era it was the residence for the first missionary school and it was a major port. This centre is also famed for being a genuine city under the sea! The myths of sunken cities have captivated many imaginations, yet we discovered that parts of this metropolis are still lost under water. Once a diver was in the bay of Alexandria and out of the watery haze he saw the face of a pharaoh looking directly at him! Alexandria suffered from earthquakes and subsidence that forced parts of the ancient city to sink into the sea. In the bay today are the remains of Cleopatra's palace and the great lighthouse. Some of the city's relics have now been brought to the surface and rest in the Open Air Museum, by the Roman Coliseum.

Excavations at Alexandria still continue, but the trail for the Ark of the Covenant had gone cold. So it was expedient for us to travel back into the relics of the New Kingdom of ancient Egypt and enter the tomb of the world's most famous pharaoh to search for leads.

Tutankhamun's Gold
'The treasures of gold and silver...all the precious things of Egypt' Daniel 11:43.

When we entered Tutankhamun's tomb in the Valley of the Kings, in Luxor, we were astonished at how little this sepulchre is. Compared to many other tombs, the primary chamber is about the size of a garage. Pharaoh Tutankhamun was only a teenager when he died and with over three hundred pharaohs in Egyptian history, he was quickly forgotten by most. In fact, his low profile in Egyptian history is the reason why the antiquities of his tomb were kept safely buried underground; the thieves forgot about this insignificant pharaoh! Beyond the entrance corridor, this world famous tomb has four main chambers - of critical value to us were the burial chamber and the treasury. The intact tomb of Tutankhamun was discovered in 1922, after years of diligent excavation by the archaeologist Howard Carter. The golden treasures found inside are now on display in the Egyptian Museum. Visitors rush to see his famous golden facemask, but the antiquity that caught our eyes was the Portable Simulacrum of Anubis, for its similarity to the Bible's Ark of the Covenant! With a little computer cultivation, we saw how this gold plated wooden box could be transformed! First remove the doglike Anubis, then overlay the worn Egyptian golden symbols with a bright golden covering and finally add an artist's impression of the two cherubim.

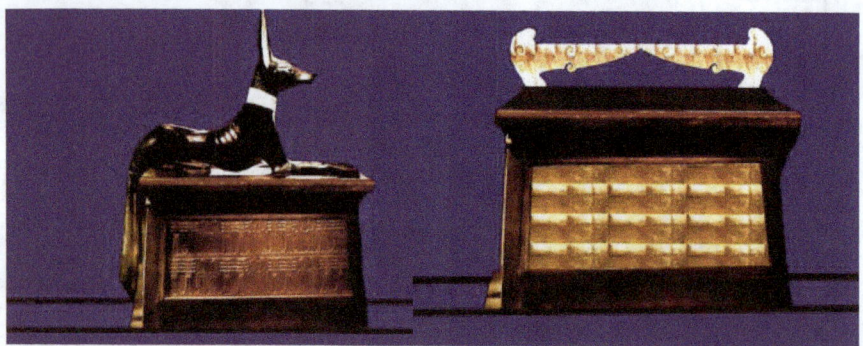

Moses was trained in ancient Egypt and Tutankhamun's funeral hoard proves that sacred boxes, covered with gold and carried with poles were familiar to Egyptians. As we established what the Ark's literal image may have looked like, we had to proceed to examine the historical record to find out what happened to the Ark, and ask if it still exists, after over three millennia since its creation.

The Antiquities of the Second Temple
"I say to you that in this place there is One greater than the Temple" Matthew 12:6.

If our inquiry is to detect what happened to the Ark of the Covenant, we must ask when was the last time articles from the Temple of Jerusalem were seen and visually recorded for posterity? To do this, we must look back many years to our travels to Rome, Italy. The great coliseum in Rome is spectacular, yet how many people know that it was partly funded by the destruction of Judea?

In 70AD, Titus with his father's blessing completed his objective to take Jerusalem; the Temple was destroyed and the sacred artefacts inside were stolen. Jesus' prophecy had come true, Matthew 24:2. Many Jews were sold as slaves and profit from this campaign helped pay for the coliseum. Titus catalogued his war on a triumphal arch in Rome and his memorial contains an incredible depiction.

This is the equivalent of a two thousand year old photo of the sacred biblical treasures from the Temple which Jesus once preached in, Ezra 6:5, Matthew 21:12. Clearly visible is the seven-branched golden menorah, the silver trumpets and possibly the jewel covered table of Divine Presence, Exodus 25:31-32, Ezra 3:10, Hebrews 9.

Almost two millennia later, this monument allows us to look inside the Holy Temple of Jerusalem and see the objects that are listed in the Bible! The Romans took the Temple treasure to their capital and this record proves beyond contradiction that the articles mentioned in the Bible were verifiable objects. This incredible chronicle is the closest we can get to literally seeing inside Jerusalem's Temple! Conspicuously absent from the memorial is the Ark. This chronicle therefore indicates the Ark was never captured by Rome and scholars agree with considerable certainty that the Ark was never in the Second Temple. But what happened to these Jewish treasures?

It is estimated that Vespasian looted fifty tons of gold from the Jews; much of this was used to pay for building projects and soldiers; but the vessels from Herod's Temple were publicly displayed and later stored. Josephus wrote in the first century that Vespasian erected a Temple of Peace in Rome and inside 'he laid up the vessels of gold from the Temple of the Jews.' In 455AD, Rome was looted by the Vandals, their temples were emptied and ships sailed to Carthage (Tunisia) with the booty. Almost eighty years later, the Byzantine Emperor Justinian defeated the Vandals, bringing back glory to the new Roman Empire. He also brought back the treasure of the Jews; for Procopius chronicled that in Constantinople these vessels were displayed including 'the treasures of the Jews, which Titus, the son of Vespasian...had brought to Rome after the capture of Jerusalem.'

The emperor Justinian had some form of Christian faith and a fear of God to go with it. Procopius attests that a Jew in his court saw the Temple vessels and said, "These treasures, I think it inexpedient (a mistake) to carry them into the palace of Byzantium. Indeed it is not possible for them to be elsewhere than in the place where Solomon, the King of the Jews formerly placed them." Then he warned Justinian that every empire which held these treasures soon fell. In fear of offending God Justinian 'sent everything to the sanctuary of the Christians in Jerusalem.' The Church of the Holy Sepulchre was the most prestigious, so if this account can be trusted, the Second Temple vessels arrived back in Jerusalem around 550AD. Just over six decades later, in 614AD, Persian armies invaded Jerusalem and a document called *The Khuzistan Chronicle* details that thieves dug into the Church of the Holy Sepulchre looking for the articles, but did not find them. The Second Temple treasures had disappeared. Since then many have proposed locations, churches, monasteries and empires that took the vessels, but no genuine leads have been forthcoming. Some believe that the coming Islamic conquests led to them being melted down, others state that they are locked inside the Vatican vaults and in 1996 Israel's Religious Affairs Minister officially asked for their return. The Vatican denied ever possessing them. On a positive note, these chronicles and the Scriptures indicate that in antiquity, the victors of wars paraded the captured treasures of other peoples and stored them in a splurge of self-indulgence. This gives us hope that the Ark of the Covenant, if ever captured, was not dismantled and melted down for its gold. Could it still be out there?

Pharaoh Shishak's Invasion of Judah
'Shishak King of Egypt came up against Jerusalem and he took away the treasures of the house of the Lord' 1 Kings 14:25-26.

In the time of Solomon, a Temple was erected in ancient Israel to be a permanent residence for the Ark of the Covenant, 1 Kings 5-8; but five years after Solomon's death, the Bible chronicles that the Temple was raided by Pharaoh Shishak. If we can find the Egyptian account of this campaign, perhaps we can find some clues to discover what happened to the treasures from Solomon's Temple.

We hired some bikes for the day, to give us access to places off the tourist routes and our intention paid dividends. As we cycled, we noticed Egyptian relics and broken sphinxes on the waste ground, away from the road. We followed these splintered remains, until we turned a corner to find an ancient paved road, with an avenue of sphinxes stationed on both sides as far as the eye could see. We were far away from the main tourist entrance to the Temple of Karnack and this avenue was quiet, almost abandoned. We anticipated seeing groups of tourists around the corner, yet instead we found another empty road, leading to a large temple entrance. We had literally stumbled

upon this almost abandoned entrance to the Karnack complex and we felt like one of the first explorers, who by accident had found a lost temple. These sphinxes once joined the Temple of Luxor in the centre of town, to the very large Temple of Karnack and it was these dilapidated remains which we had unintentionally followed.

The Bible immortalises in the sacred text that a pharaoh called Shishak invaded Judah and took away the treasures of Solomon's Temple. In our research we identified that Shishak is the Hebrew translation of the name Sheshonq. Consequently in the Temple of Karnack we scoured for any references to or by Pharaoh Sheshonq I. Then in an incredible confirmation of Scripture, we found the story of Egypt's invasion of the land of Canaan on a wall in this temple!

Though this relief is gravely damaged, its original intent was to represent Pharaoh Sheshonq I and the god Amun taking captive the enemies of Egypt.

By studying this Egyptian record of the campaign of Sheshonq I, Egyptologists have been able to use this data to draw up a possible route which this pharaoh may have taken. Several of the places identified on the wall can still be found today, yet lamentably many names have been badly damaged and are now unreadable. Jerusalem is missing from the wall, but the route indicates it was on the itinerary as the Bible

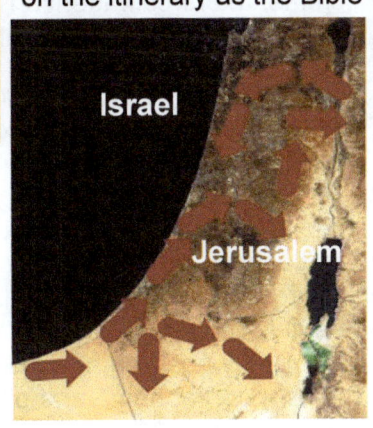

confirms. Evidence for this campaign has also been traced on an Egyptian relief in Megiddo, Israel. Having identified confirmation of the Bible's description of Shishak's invasion of the land, we wondered if it would be possible to find out what this man did with the riches of Solomon's Temple!

> **The Silver of Solomon's Temple**
> 'They will be (Shishak's) servants, that they may distinguish My service from the service of the kingdoms of the nations' 2 Chron. 12:8.

Could it be possible to track down the gold and silver that came from Solomon's Temple? Could you imagine seeing the wealth that once rested inside Israel's first Temple! This was a captivating concept.

When Solomon reigned, the Bible indicates that Israel arrived at its greatest peak, with mountains of wealth and an empire. During the same time, Egypt was in a long period of decline, for the glory days of the New Kingdom were far behind and Egypt was struggling in their Third Intermediate Period. Plunder became more important to the weakened Egypt and the Bible states that the fame of Solomon's wealth had spread throughout the world, 1 Kings 10, 2 Chronicles 12:9. Between these two nations, the small and wealthy Israel and the inadequate Egypt entered Jeroboam. In his pride, Solomon had forsaken the Lord, and a prophet told Jeroboam that the nation of Israel would be divided and he would lead ten tribes. Upon hearing this Solomon sought to kill Jeroboam and he fled to Pharaoh Shishak in Egypt, 1 Kings 11:29-40. No doubt the tidings of political instability in Israel were great news for Shishak because there was a great deal of wealth in Jerusalem. Jewish experts who have studied the wealth of Israel during the age of David and Solomon have summarised that the Bible describes them having many thousands of tons of gold and silver, 1 Kings 6-7, 1 Chronicles 28 and 29, 2 Chronicles 2-4. When scholars question the Bible's account, commentators call attention to Alexander the Great who took huge amounts of gold from ancient kingdoms in his campaigns.

After Solomon's death, Jeroboam left Egypt and returned to Israel to present the case for a tax cut for the people, after the late king's expensive building campaigns. The new king ignored the plea and alienated his people, causing the split of the Kingdom into Israel and Judah, 1 Kings 11:29-12:19. This division fundamentally weakened the capacity of the Jews to defend themselves from any military threat. Meanwhile, the wealth of the Jews was tantalising for any foreign power and Shishak's war machine was soon entering the land. Every pharaoh needed a successful military campaign to boost their support at home and plunder from foreign people would help to pacify Egypt's troubles. Some scholars believe that Judah was so weak that they could not fight and they gave Shishak Solomon's treasures to save the Temple. But where did he take their riches?

The next phase in our investigation was to travel to Tanis, the city where Shishak launched his attack on Judah and the place where his sons were buried. However, could archaeologists ever find any gold or silver here? Grave robbers are sometimes as infamous as the pharaohs, for they managed to search out and empty the royal tombs of their wealth. In fact, the situation was so bad that Egyptian priests eventually gathered and hid away the mummified bodies of their pharaohs in order to protect them. Pharaoh Shishak's tomb and the wealth within have never been found. No leads there then. Nevertheless in Tanis riches were uncovered second only to Tutankhamun's; yet the discovery was never made famous for this excavation took place during WWII, when the world had bigger problems to think about and the finds were only published in French.

Tanis was the burial ground for the successors of the pharaoh who attacked Jerusalem and just fifty years after his death, Pharaoh Osorkon II came to power. We entered his tomb, with many others besides and we chanced upon a window into the ancient world.

The Bible declares that Shishak took the wealth of Jerusalem and Egyptians were always working on projects, including burial deposits which needed gold and silver. Therefore was any of Solomon's treasure melted down and recast to be buried in these royal tombs? Many of the antiquities of Jerusalem were taken by Shishak and when archaeologists excavated these tombs, they identified golden treasures that the grave robbers had missed. Inside they dug up a bracelet bearing the name of Sheshonq I, the man who took Judah's wealth and his relatives were buried with gold and silver. Sheshonq II had a golden face mask and a large silver coffin. When Solomon reigned he boasted of the abundance of silver in Jerusalem, but after his death Egypt plundered the nation, 2 Chronicles 9:10-27.

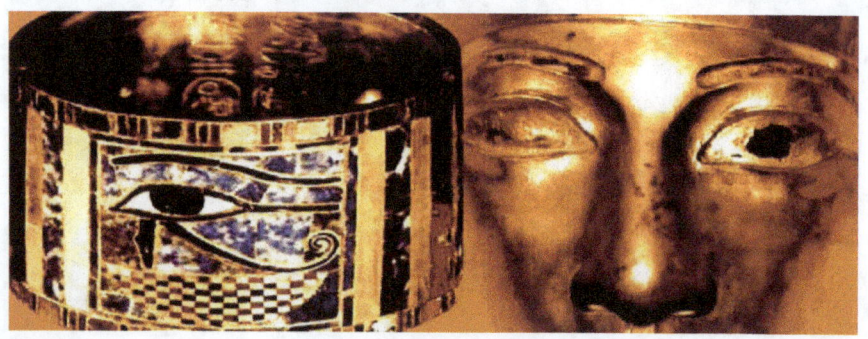

Our next stop was at the Egyptian Museum the new home of these relics which were buried for over two and half millennia. In the Tanis exhibit, next to Tutankhamun's display, we stood speechless gazing at the bracelet worn by the pharaoh who entered Jerusalem and took the wealth from Israel's first Temple! How many Christians visit this museum without realising that the man who wore this bracelet saw Solomon's Temple? Two steps away, we found the silver coffin and the golden facemask. These discoveries are almost unknown to the public and whilst experts cannot prove that these antiquities were made with Jerusalem's wealth, the link remains provocative.

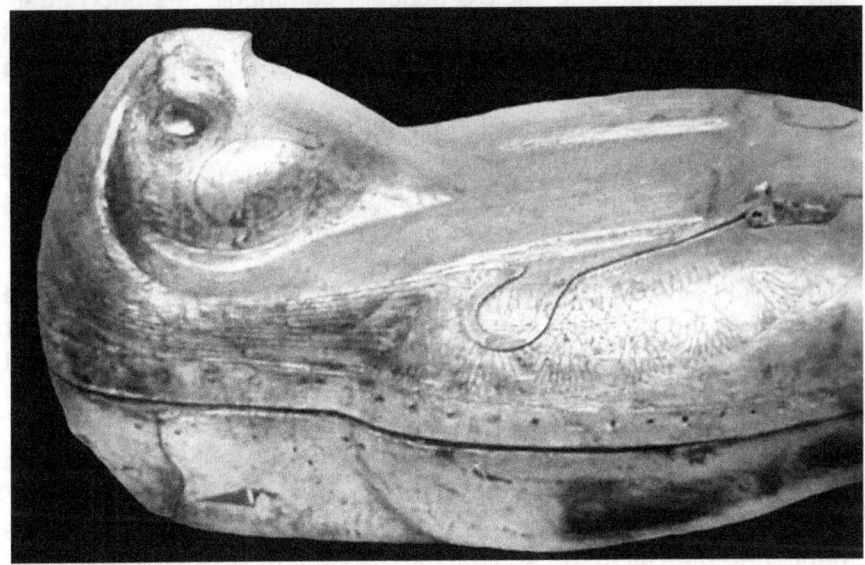

When we ask what happened to the wealth of Solomon's Temple, the Bible gives us the answer. One of the culprits who stripped the Temple was Shishak, and plunder from his campaign would have been used to build his memorial in the Temple of Karnack and some of Jerusalem's gold and silver may have been recast, and buried in Tanis. But did Shishak take the Ark of the Covenant? The Bible chronicles that he took many Temple articles, yet it suggests that other holy items must have been left, with the Ark itself being one such object, 2 Kings 24:13-14, 25:8-17. For the priests of Jerusalem the Ark of the Covenant and other sacred items were not pawns to be traded in for a short-term peace - the Ark was where God Himself dwelt, Leviticus 16:2, Num. 7:89. Also, the Bible confirms that the Ark did not go with Shishak, for it records the Ark being in Jerusalem many centuries later, 2 Chronicles 35:3. Therefore Egypt's Shishak did not gain possession of the Ark of the Covenant.

The Jews in Egyptian Records

'The Lord has said concerning you, O remnant of Judah, "Do not go down to Egypt!"'
Jeremiah 42:19.

In our last investigation to find the exodus evidence, we learnt that Egypt acknowledged the existence of the ancient people of Israel 1,200 years before Christ. Sheshonq's report of the invasion of the land combined with the Bible's account communicates once again that Egyptians and the people of the Bible coexisted in the ancient world of historical fact. However, in all of Egypt's chronicles we have only been able to find one direct reference to the name Israel. This conundrum presents the sincere possibility that Israel and Judah may have been cited many times in Egyptian history using a generic name for Semitic people, and it could also indicate that Egyptians used another name for the Jews which is still unknown.

The Bible and Egyptian history agree that Shishak invaded the land, yet in the Egyptian narrative we do not find the name Israel or Judah. For the Jews, the invasion of the land was a traumatic event worthy of note, but for the Egyptians God's people were just one of many weaker kingdoms that needed to be put in their place. Unfortunately, the relief of Shishak's invasion is terribly damaged, to the extent that the depiction of this pharaoh has been destroyed. Therefore, it could be the case that Judah and Jerusalem were mentioned directly in the substantial areas of this damage relief. Yet we are fortunate that this memorial of Shishak's war stands as another incredible confirmation of the accuracy of biblical history.

Nonetheless, it is still a mystery why Egyptian history proves they acknowledged the existence of the people of Israel in the land for over 1,200 years and still in all of that time, they chose only once to directly indicate their presence! Some have proposed this was a political ploy by the Egyptians. For ancient Egypt, the land of Canaan was their area of influence, often within Egypt's direct control. This land was their colony, part of their empire and the Bible's description of the Jewish presence in the land appears to confirm that for most of their existence, God's people were pawns in the game of other powers. Therefore, the suggestion has been made that by refusing to directly acknowledge the Kingdom of Israel and Judah, Egypt was reassessing its claim to Canaan. Perhaps we can hear their empire builders stating, "The Kingdoms of Israel and Judah do not exist; only Egypt's right to the land exists." Three and a half millennia later, most of the neighbours of modern Israel still apply this method to disenfranchise the Jews.

The ancient Hebrews throughout much of their history were effectively second-class citizens in their own nation, and other empires made them realise they were the weak subjects of foreign powers, in a land which they had claimed for their own.

We don't sufficiently understand why the ancient Egyptians made only one direct reference to the people of Israel and their descendants, but we can confirm that for over one thousand years, the nation of Egypt knew that a people called Israel were living in the land. Also, in the case of Shishak and other biblical events Egypt's chronicle adds credence to the Scriptural narrative. There may be more details of the Jews to be detected in Egyptian accounts and with three millennia passing, some of these may have been destroyed. Fortunately, we do have the records of many other peoples and nations, who recognised and immortalised the existence of the people of the Bible in their reliefs.

The Trail of Jerusalem's Wealth
'All the articles from the house of God…and the treasures of the king and of his leaders… he took to Babylon' 2 Chronicles 36:18.

The Bible specifically states that God made the Jews the servants of Pharaoh Shishak in order to teach them the difference between serving a foreign power, to serving Him faithfully, 2 Chronicles 12:8. This lesson should have taught them that it is better to be righteous, faithful to the Lord and free, rather than being wicked, backslidden and a slave to a foreign power. However, the people of the Bible failed to listen to their prophets and refused spiritual instruction.

Ancient Egypt was a major player in the story of Israel, yet as with all the great civilisations, it declined as other powers arose. We arrived in the Valley of the Queens in Luxor, to enter a new set of tombs. In this area many powerful people were buried who saw Egypt's finest hour, but also others witnessed the long period of decline that led to Egypt's retreat from Canaan. The long heyday of Egypt changed history, but as it weakened, other nations both great and small, quickly became a threat to Israel and Judah. The Bible documents that Solomon's Temple, the home of the Ark, was plundered many times by these peoples and by studying the Bible we can learn what happened to Solomon's treasures. The Scriptures bear witness that articles from Jerusalem were taken to Egypt, (1 Kings 14:25-26), Syria (1 Kings 15:18, 2 Kg. 12:18, 2 Chronicles 16:2), Assyria (2 Kg. 16:8, 17-20, 18:15), Arabia, (2 Chron. 21:16-17), Babylon (2 Kings 24:13-14, 25:8-19, 2 Chronicles 36:10,18, Dn. 1:2), Sidon, Tyre, Philistia (Joel 3:4-5) and woefully the King of Israel plundered the Temple (2 Kg. 14:12-14, 2 Chron. 25:22-24). Nevertheless, none of these biblical accounts record that the Ark was taken.

When Egypt was deteriorating as a power, the Bible announced the rise of the Assyrian threat to Judah and Israel, 2 Chronicles 32, and in an astonishing validation of biblical history an Assyrian relief confirms these events and gives us the only representation of a King of Israel! This is Jehu King of Israel, anointed by the prophet Elijah

and according to the Bible made subject to Assyria because of Israel's sins, 1 Kings 19. 'But Jehu took no heed to walk in the law of the Lord God of Israel' 2 Kings 10:31. This Black Obelisk affirms the Bible's account of ancient history, and there are many other artefacts that support the Bible's description of the following years - including the Babylonian Chronicle of Years 605-594BC which validates that Assyria was later surpassed by Babylon and that Judah was invaded by the Babylonians, 2 Kings 24, 2 Chronicles 36, Daniel 1. The Bible states that 'Nebuchadnezzar King of Babylon came against the city' of Jerusalem, 2 Kings 24:11. 'Then they burned down the house of God...and the treasures...he took to Babylon' 2 Chronicles 36:18-19. Jeremiah the prophet lived through these days and just before the Babylonian invasion his chronicle indicates that the Ark of the Covenant was still in Jerusalem, Jeremiah 3:16. Nevertheless, in 586BC, Solomon's Temple was destroyed by the Babylonians and the Ark of the Covenant disappeared from the pages of history.

Jeremiah registered that many Jews escaped into Egypt at this time and some believe that the Ark of the Covenant left Jerusalem for safety in Egypt, just before the fall of King Solomon's Temple, Jeremiah 42-46. But where did these Jews go in Egypt? Are

there any Jewish settlements in Egypt where they could have fled?

A Lost Jewish Temple

'In that day there will be an altar to the Lord in the midst of the land of Egypt and a pillar to the Lord at its border' Isaiah 19:19.

We studied the Scriptures to learn where the Jews lived in Egypt and we found that Isaiah wrote that in his lifetime many Jews were already settled in Sinim, which is an area around Aswan, Isaiah 49:12. Did the fleeing Jews come here? In Aswan, we looked for any leads to help us find the evidence for an ancient Jewish community being near. We visited the tombs of the Nobles, overlooking Aswan, but we detected nothing helpful, so we hired a boat to sail on the Nile. As we sailed on the river, our eyes were drawn sumptuously toward Elephantine Island and it was on this very settlement that a very exciting discovery was made. Archaeologists uncovered a large collection of ancient Jewish manuscripts dating to around 500 years before Christ, proving that a Jewish community once lived at this site. To the amazement of many, a letter called the Petition to Bagoas confirmed that a Jewish temple once stood on this island in Egypt! The letter stated it was called the Temple of Yahweh and the Passover Letter certified that the priests carried out animal and grain sacrifices, whilst observing the Passover as Moses instructed. Using the data available from the archaeological remains at the site, we constructed an artist's impression of this Jewish temple.

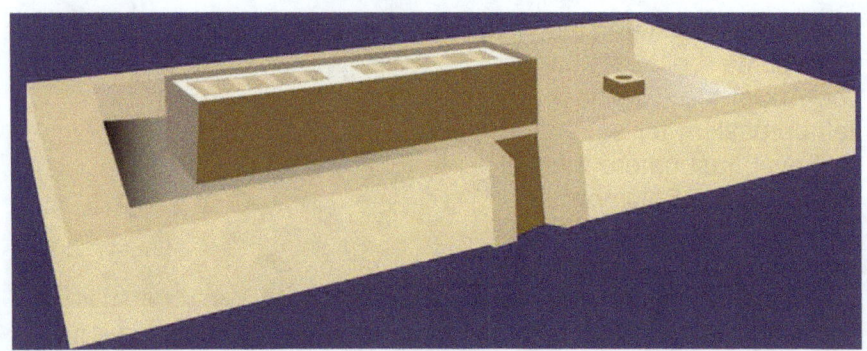

Why was there a Jewish temple in Egypt? The Bible indicates that the primary purpose for building the original temple was to house the Ark of the Covenant, so was this temple built for the same purpose? 1 Chronicles 17:1. When Jewish scholars examined the remains of this temple, they discovered it was very similar in size to the Tabernacle of Moses, and this was never designed to be the final resting place for the Ark of the Covenant. Instead the Ark stayed in the Tabernacle whilst God's people hoped for a permanent sanctuary to be built in their land, Deuteronomy 12:11,14. We also determined from these letters that this Jewish community was in contact with the captives who were returning after the exile to Jerusalem, for they note Johanan a Levite and Sanballat; both men are cited in the Bible, Neh. 2:19, 12:23. Consequently, this provides independent verification of the Bible's account of these characters!

Jeremiah prophesied trouble for the Jews in Egypt and the Petition to Bagoas confirmed that disorder did come, for the temple was 'burned to the ground...in the fourteenth year of Darius,' and, 'as for the basins of gold and silver and other articles that were in the temple' the Egyptians 'carried all of them off' Jeremiah 44:13-14. It's not possible to prove the Ark was once in this lost Jewish temple, but if the Levite priests did flee Jerusalem to keep the Ark safe, then this is the only location that meets the biblical requirements for its safe keeping. Secondly, its presence would compare favourable with legends that the Ark was taken south for its own safety. If the Ark formerly resided in this temple, it had to be moved before its destruction, and we were told that because of the turmoil in Jerusalem and Egypt, the only safe place for the Ark was south, with the Jewish communities in Africa, Zephaniah 3:10, Acts 8:27. Therefore, if this temple was used to keep the Ark secure, it would have arrived before the fall of Solomon's Temple in 586BC and moved on before 407BC, when this Jewish temple was destroyed. In consequence, we had to study the Bible and Egyptian chronicles to find any Kingdoms south of Egypt where the Ark may have gone.

Pharaoh Hatshepsut's Mission to Africa
'A man of Ethiopia...of great authority...had come to Jerusalem to worship' Acts 8:27.

The Bible unveils there were numerous great African Kingdoms in the ancient world; sadly many were lost in the sands of time. Thus we went to Hatshepsut's Temple in Luxor, to evaluate Egypt's greatest relief of a lost African Kingdom, 2 Kings 19:9, 2 Chronicles 14:9. In this temple the female Pharaoh Hatshepsut details a historic expedition on the Red Sea to a land she called Punt. Stepping back around 3,500 years, these carvings allow us to visualise a lost African Kingdom! These depictions even portray an image of a leader of this forgotten African land, calling her Queen Ity.

Egyptian reliefs of the land of Punt exemplify the types of homes that these Africans resided in over three millennia ago. Who were the people that lived in these dwellings and where was this land located? Pharaoh Hatshepsut took seven great ships to the land of Punt, to bring back incense trees and other precious items. These illustrations indicate it was a large trading venture and as we examined them, we realised these records were consistent with the Bible's account of the Kingdom of Sheba.

Hundreds of years after this trip, the Queen of Sheba, who came from a land south of Israel, visited Solomon and they exchanged gifts like those engraved here, Luke 11:31. The Bible divulges that the Queen of Sheba gave Solomon 'gold, spices in great quantity and precious stones' 1 Kings 10:10. Experts who have studied the Bible's account of the land of Sheba have concluded there are two primary locations where it could have been located. One is in the region of Yemen, the other is the horn of Africa in or by Ethiopia. Those who have studied this region became aware that the empires based in this part of the world have ruled parts of Yemen and Ethiopia at the same time. Could this be the Bible's land of Sheba? Jesus Himself indicated that Sheba was a land very far away and was south of Israel saying, "The Queen of the south...came from the ends of the earth to hear the wisdom of Solomon" Matthew 12:42.

As we pondered these matters, we discovered that some scholars have identified that the descriptions of the land of Punt and Sheba are both consistent with the nation of Ethiopia. This theory suggests that hundreds of years after the Egyptian visit to the land of Punt, the nation evolved into the kingdom of Sheba. This concept was very interesting to us, because millions of people believe a legend that the Ark of the Covenant was smuggled by Levite priests into Ethiopia around the time of the Queen of Sheba.

Are these stories which we heard serious historical accounts or just myths? Our mission was to investigate these leads to discover if they had any basis in fact. To do this, we had to sail up the River Nile into Sudan and cross the desert into Ethiopia.

Egypt, Sudan and Ethiopia
'Fear not, for I am with you. Be not dismayed, for I am your God' Isaiah 41:10.

We queued up at the ferry port, the only one between Egypt and Sudan and saw a scene that you would expect to witness in a film set in the nineteenth century. Hundreds of people were crowded around, shouting in various languages, with large packages and containers on their heads. There was a rush for tickets and traders ran onto the ship, hoping to find any space for their goods before it was full. On the slope before the ferry, a man lost control of his heavy laden two wheeled cart and chased it as it ploughed towards the crowd below. Eight hours later, we were still docked, with boxes, barrels and an unknown quantity of goods bursting from every space. We walked around the deck and witnessed that ninety-eight percent of the passengers were locals. There was a good reason why tourists weren't planning their holiday in the Sudan. Just a few months before an English teacher was arrested for a perceived insult to Islam and the extremists called for her to be beheaded. Only careful negotiation by the moderates secured her release. With this story still fresh in our minds from the news, we went to sleep as

we sailed towards the border. In the morning, we awoke still in Egyptian waters. On the deck we saw our last glimpse of Egypt, as we sailed past the four statues of Ramesses II at Abu-Simbel, the historic boundary between ancient Egypt and the Nubian Kingdom. Several hours later we came close to the border and everybody on deck was forced to go inside as a Sudanese boat was on its way to inspect us. Out of the distance, a vessel with armed guards onboard sped towards us and landed. The atmosphere felt very tense and we wondered if we had made a mistake in coming. A few hours later, we docked and took our first look out of the window. We saw a guard, wearing blacked out glasses and a hardened stare on his face. Fortunately, our cloak and dagger ordeal transformed as a friendly team of bureaucrats arrived onboard to check the passports of the few foreigners, and led us to a four-wheeled vehicle that sped through the dust into a settlement. That night we slept in a sandy ghost-community in the desert and awoke for the two day train ride on a hard seat to Khartoum. In the capital, we had to register with the government as foreigners and paid a large fee for the pleasure. Five days later, we were in a small vehicle leaving the nation with many locals, and at a checkpoint one woman had faulty documents and she was removed. We then crossed with some relief out of Sudan and into Ethiopia. On the border, no-one spoke English, but the kind locals directed us to a small hut where eight of us slept. We were on the trail of the Ark and it was taking us into the unknown!

The Jews of Ethiopia
'It was written…to the Jews…from India to Ethiopia' Esther 8:9.

The Bible illustrates that there was a large Jewish community in Ethiopia long before the time of Christ. We cannot confirm where the borders of Ethiopia were in those days, as they are subject to change; nonetheless it is evident that this Jewish tradition can still be observed in Ethiopia today. The New Testament also confirms that practising Jews were in prominent positions in Ethiopia and that Ethiopian Jews began to embrace Christ as Messiah, Acts 8:27.

Ethiopia is the land of lost civilisations, mentioned in the Bible, recorded in ancient literature and re-discovered by archaeologists. Yet of all the mysteries of this land, only one tale takes us back to the story of the lost Ark of the Covenant. As we questioned the Ethiopians about it, they told us with certainty that Ethiopia gained possession of the Ark several millennia ago. If their claim is true, how did they get it? Our first thought was of the Jewish temple that we found in Elephantine, Egypt. Did Levite priests take the Ark from that temple and smuggle it into Ethiopia during that era of war and crisis? However, the Ethiopians alleged they had the Ark of the Covenant a long time before the construction of that temple. In fact, their claim goes all the way back to the time of Solomon! We knew that we needed to find an original source document to confirm what and why the Ethiopians believe these things, so after doing some research, we realised we needed to find an ancient book called the *Kebra Nagast* - Ethiopia's book of the Glory of Kings. We wanted to

examine the oldest surviving copy available; but lamentably a fire had devastated the aged monastery containing these; so we came to the third highest capital in the world, Addis Ababa, to inspect an old rock church, located at

the highest peak of the capital. We hired a taxi to go to the church on Mount Entoto, but the elevation led it to overheat and after a few hours of breakdowns, we arrived and arranged to see the famous *Kebra Nagast*.

According to this book, after the Queen of Sheba visited Solomon in Israel, she returned back to Ethiopia to find she was pregnant with his son. Years later the child called Menelik, went to Israel to see his father and after witnessing the backsliding of Solomon, he left under the cover of darkness taking the Ark of the Covenant with him to Ethiopia, where it still resides today! Immediately we sensed some inconsistencies with this story and as this legend is not found in the Bible, it needs to be tested thoroughly. It would be easy to quickly dismiss this Ethiopian claim because of the contradictions we found, however we must recall that this is the only nation on earth that has a religion which is still centred on the Ark of the Covenant. Every Ethiopian Orthodox church possesses a replica of the Ark in a part of their sanctuary which they call the Holy of Holies, and it is central to their worship. These facts imply that at some point in history the Ethiopians obtained 'an Ark', but was it 'the Ark?' After pondering this, our immediate hypothesis was that the Ethiopian Ark of the Covenant could have arrived from four sources. 1. Levite priests from the temple of Elephantine in Egypt smuggled the Ark from their temple

to this nation. 2. An Ethiopian emperor had a replica Ark made and alleged it to be real, to substantiate his claim to the throne. 3. The Jewish communities in Ethiopia built an Ark, as they were unable to worship back in Jerusalem. 4. The Ethiopian legend of the Queen of Sheba's son bringing the original Ark to this nation has validity.

We also visited many other churches in Addis Ababa, including this one to view other copies of their holy book. In every church and city we found that the Ethiopian Christians believed in Sheba's legend. However, the account of her having a son with Solomon and the Ark being brought into this nation is not found in the Bible. Therefore we had to examine these legends by visiting the remains of the ancient and forgotten civilisations of Ethiopia!

Underground Rock Churches

'From beyond the rivers of Ethiopia, My worshippers, the daughter of My dispersed ones (the Jews), shall bring My offering' Zep. 3:10.

Our mission to find the forgotten and overlooked Ethiopia began at Gondar, where we discovered buildings that we never imagined we would find in this nation. This is Africa's Camelot, which dates to the sixteen hundreds and these castles echo Ethiopia's Christian and Jewish heritage. As we explored them, we found many references in the architecture to Ethiopia's biblical aspirations, but if we were to examine the legend of the regal Queen of Sheba, we would need to go back further in  time. Our next stop led us back almost one millennia to the world heritage site of the underground rock churches of Lalibela.

It took several days on a bus to make it near to this area. Ethiopian roads, where they exist, still consist of tiny stones scattered over the reclaimed scrubland and the buses tend to move very fast. The texture of the majority of these roads is ribbed, like a thousand mini  speed bumps blended into their very fabric. This resulted in us spending day after day being shaken around like a NASA test pilot, and behind the bus a trail of dust blew up into the air giving any poor passerby an unwanted dust bath.

With the insistent shaking of the bus, came the unfortunate re-occurring incident of the man who sat three rows in front of us. Above his small body were several large bags, which every few minutes would shake out of place and crash onto his head, to the amusement of many. The only foreigner we met was a Korean, who after a few days of travel on another bus, fell violently ill and spent a small fortune to hire a seat in a four-wheeled drive vehicle to exit the nation in comfort. It is possible for wealthy foreigners to visit these sites using a small aircraft, but that was not an option for us. Anyway, after all this travel the final destination proved itself worthy.

The rock churches of Lalibela are one of the wonders of the world. Built in the twelfth century, these eleven underground churches were cut out of solid rock and sunk fifty feet below the surface. It's estimated that the builders had to move 150,000 tons of rock over two decades to complete this project, and therefore we had to explore this labyrinth of tunnels and sealed mazes. This complex took us back in time to a lost age, locked inside Ethiopia and the priests inside claim to know where the original Ark is hidden.

In 1187AD, the Islamic armies took Jerusalem and it soon became impossible for any Christian to make a pilgrimage to the city. In this context, Ethiopia's King Lalibela claimed he received a vision from God to build a new Jerusalem. Experts who have examined this complex suggest that in part, it was built like an underground fortress to protect these Christians from the threat of Islamic invasion, which did come later. As we walked down the steps and entered into the underground labyrinth of the Lalibela churches, we distinctly saw the chisel marks made by the labourers who only had primitive tools to use. This endeavour is unparalleled. We found many tunnels leading in every direction, some to the village and others to the water supply. In some areas, the tunnel system has not yet been opened and explored. In one part we were in complete darkness, until the light at the end of the tunnel pointed upwards to another church. Inside the priests were praying, chanting and carefully guarding the legacy of the Ark.

Within these churches we identified many Jewish and Christian symbols and some believe this could have been the perfect hiding place for the Ark of the Covenant; but now only a replica resides in each church. Yet, if we could examine a replica, we could learn if it meets the biblical criteria for the Ark. However the priests indicated this was not possible; for the Ark is too holy to be seen by outsiders.

Every Ethiopian Orthodox church contains a replica of the Ark of the Covenant in a part of their sanctuary which they call the Holy of Holies. However, only the priests are allowed to go beyond the curtain to be near it. This veil separates the worshipper from the holy place and from a replica of the Ark. In every underground church, we found ourselves confronted with the veil, guaranteeing that no one could see a replica of their Ark. But suddenly we found a church where the curtain was left partially open and so I looked beyond the veil into their holiest place! Inside the Holy of Holies, I saw a rectangular container covered with a cloth being used as an altar. It was smaller than the biblical description of the Ark; there were no cherubim on top and the rings for carrying it were absent. This was the closest we had been to Ethiopia's Ark of the Covenant, yet we couldn't get close enough to study it. We wanted to get near to the original Ark and the priests told us that the genuine Ark now resides in the sacred town of Axum. Our quest therefore continued onto this ancient site. What would we find?

A Lost African Civilisation
For Moses 'had married an Ethiopian woman' Numbers 12:1.

The Bible testifies that during periods in history Ethiopia played a role in biblical events; Ethiopians fought in some of the wars of the Bible and Moses married an Ethiopian. As we have already explained it is not possible to verify the actual borders of ancient Ethiopia for nations grow and contract, encompassing various people groups and lands. It may be the case that at times the land translated as Ethiopia in the Bible could be describing another people group in the region. Nevertheless the Scriptures do suggest that great kingdoms were located in this region and with this lead, we should be able to discover a substantial wealth of archaeological information in this land. After another bus journey we arrived in Axum and we soon began to find the relics of an ancient empire, fallen by the side of the road where it had collapsed centuries before.

Up until the twentieth century, few knew of this empire, except for brief vague references in antiquity and biblical records of a kingdom, Acts 8:27. Yet, by the hard work of archaeologists we began to uncover the lost Aksumite civilisation. Axum was once the capital of an empire which ruled this region from 400BC. until the tenth century. The most obvious legacy is the one hundred plus obelisks, most probably markers for the royal tombs of antiquity, which once contained outstanding riches of their age. In this obscure empire we found the largest monolith standing stone of the ancient world, which weighs up to five hundred tons and was cut from a single piece of stone. This nation had a language called Geez and they minted their own coins, which have been dug up as far away as India. These coins also provide archaeological data which give us a timeline for the religious shift from pagan worship to Christianity; for the pagan motif of a crescent was replaced with a cross. Our most important viewing was the Ezana Stone, a very large ancient memorial written in Greek, Sabaean (southern Arabian) and Geez. This is Ethiopia's Rosetta Stone! This aged memorial immortalises the conversion of King Ezana to Christianity in the fourth century and dictates his victory over the biblical people of Kush. The Ezana Stone gives us empirical evidence for Ethiopia's transformation from pagan observance to Christianity in the fourth century and the Bible shows that some Jews began this process in the days of the apostles. To learn more about this civilisation, we began to examine ancient writings. *The Periplus of the Erythraean Sea* is a Greek manuscript which maps out the kingdoms on the Red Sea and beyond - Askum is mentioned. We also have a surviving letter from the Roman Emperor Constantius II to Axum, which indicates that Christian theologians began to be concerned that Ethiopia was straying from orthodox teaching. This letter is addressed to Ezana and asks for the head of the Ethiopian Church to visit Alexandria to contend about doctrinal errors which he held. Frumentius, their Syrian Christian leader probably never went and this appears to be the beginning of the separation of Ethiopian Christianity from the rest of the Christian world, and may be the birth of their hybrid Christianity, with its emphasis on the Ark of the Covenant. However, the evidence we have seen proves that a great civilisation was once in Axum, but nothing dates to the Queen of Sheba's time, when legend states the Ark arrived.

The Queen of Sheba's Palace?
'The Queen of Sheba heard of the fame of Solomon...and came to test him' 1 Kings 10:1.

According to Ethiopian tradition, the son of the Queen of Sheba brought the Ark of the Covenant to this nation. Before we could establish if there was any veracity to this claim, we had to ask if there is any empirical evidence that she once ruled from this region. On the outskirts of Axum, we found the reconstructed remains of a large building, called by local legend the Queen of Sheba's Palace.

We studied the research into this ancient building and upon arrival Mathew's first point to me was that this complex is still very large by comparison to the huts many Ethiopians still live in. This signals that a very rich and powerful person once lived or ruled from this compound. The excavations in addition prove this is an old structure, but how old and does it date back to the time of Solomon and Sheba? At the present, nothing has been found in this area to

prove that the Queen of Sheba was once here, or that the Ark came to this nation. In any case, we spent some time with the German archaeologist directing this excavation, and he told us that they had dug deeper than ever before and his team claimed to have detected a level dating to the time of Solomon and the Queen of Sheba. The chief archaeologist was very pleased to speak with us about his research and we exchanged details to follow up on his work. Most archaeologists still believe that a great deal of further study needs to be done in this structure before any final conclusions can be made.

We left this palace with no concrete evidence that the Queen of Sheba ever ruled in Axum and we could not find any artefacts that date to her age. The precise location of the Bible's Kingdom of Sheba is still a mystery. The Ethiopian book, called the *Kebra Nagast* contains the oldest claim that she ruled from this nation, but experts who have studied the text suggest it may only date to seven hundred years ago. This alludes to the possibility that King Ezana, with his questionable priest Frumentius, or one of their successors, devised the story of the Ark of the Covenant coming to the nation to solidify their theological and political positions.

On the famous Ezana Stone, one of the three texts engraved is the Sabaean language, and some experts have identified the similarity between the Kingdom of Saba and the recognition in the Hebrew language of the Kingdom of Sheba. The heart of this empire is found in modern Yemen, across the Red Sea from Ethiopia, and in her history, empires ruled parts of Eritrea and Ethiopia from Yemen. These people were famous traders and sold valuable items which the Queen of Sheba brought to Solomon and which were in use in Solomon's Temple, 1 Kings 10. Many of the archaeologists who have studied the question of Sheba's nation believe that discoveries made in Mareb, in Yemen, denote this is the most likely location for the Queen's Kingdom. The most convincing argument at present, is the presence of the glorified Bar'an Temple in Mareb, which indicates a wealthy kingdom existed in the land during the time of Solomon. By comparison nothing in Axum has been independently verified to date to this period. Also, monuments have been detected in the horn of Africa proving the Sabaean link.

With this new evidence available, we concluded that the legend of the Queen of Sheba may have been established in Ethiopia because of the authentic Sabaean presence in the land. Therefore, the case for the Ethiopian claim to have taken and cared for the original Ark of the Covenant is being weakened by this research. Yet, if we were to penetrate this story, we needed to be able to witness and examine the Ark itself, or at least a replica. Yet is it possible to get close to the Ethiopian Ark of the Covenant?

The Home of the Ethiopian Ark

'Then the priests brought in the Ark of the Covenant to its place, into the inner sanctuary of the Temple, to the most holy place' 1 Kings 8:6.

We have examined the case for the Ethiopian legend and we arrived at the monastery where the Ethiopians allege the Ark of the Covenant resides. At first, we walked around the modern church, where we saw another copy of the *Kebra Nagast* and we identified paintings that suggested how the Ark came to Ethiopia. One of these showed a priest carrying the Ark on his head and we immediately realised that this form of close association with the Ark was forbidden for the Levitical priests, 2 Samuel 6:6-17.

Afterwards we saw the ancient chronicles and manuscripts of this monastery, and the priests were especially interested in showing us the garments that were once worn in their ceremonies.

With our hearts stirring we walked towards the part of the complex where the priests state the original Ark of the Covenant is housed. We were informed beforehand that no-one gets to go beyond the blue gates, which separate the outer area from the inner section. Stationed by the gate was a guard, and we stopped by him and looked towards the church of the Ark. Then at the gate, we talked to one of the elders and he decided to give us permission to enter. We walked through and straight ahead we saw the home of the Ark. Just behind another set of blue gates and a blue curtain, the Ethiopians claim to possess the original Ark of the Covenant!

We were also given permission to go around to the other side of the building and for the first time we realised this was a two-story structure, giving the priest more room. We later found out that this

space was very important to him. We were told that the priest who guards the Ark has a very special privilege, and this honour comes at a cost. We asked if we could see the Ark, but we were told that only the chosen priest of this sacred sanctuary gets to be near the original Ark of the Covenant. The bricks that sealed the doorway on every side of the building are not just symbolic. Those who go beyond do so at the cost of their lives; for the priest who gets this job is forbidden to leave the sanctuary and no-one else is allowed in. This tiny blue gate is the boundary over which the priest may never step. He is both the guardian of the Ark and its prisoner. His destiny is to die behind these gates and within the last few years, every priest who has received the role of the guardian has died within two years. Some of the priests are fearful and claim that the Ark itself is radiating some power which gradually kills them. I couldn't help think that the real reason for the high mortality rate was that elderly priests are the only ones entrusted with this special role. We, like the priest in this photo, were locked outside of this sanctuary, so close yet so far. Just a few steps away from us the Ethiopian Ark of the Covenant is stored, but it was in every way out of reach. Was this a clever

tactic designed to make it impossible to verify the Ethiopian claim to the Ark, or were the priests like Israel in fear of God's judgment on those who misuse it? Beyond this fence the answers lie out of reach.

We found abundant evidence that these churches were built on ancient land, for the relics of the Aksumite Empire were buried everywhere. In addition, we saw ancient Christian monuments from a bygone age, woven into the very fabric of the new church buildings. In Axum, we saw proof of a Christian witness going back sixteen hundred years and we saw the forbidden home of the Ethiopian Ark. Yet, it seemed like our mission was ending without getting to see a replica of the Ark. We knew it would be impossible for us to see the original, but what about a copy? We then began asking around to learn if anyone knew where we could see a replica of the Ark. We were told this was most probably not possible, yet we could at least try at a small monastery at the highest point of Axum. Perhaps, if we were very fortunate the priests would allow us into the Holy of Holies to see a replica of the Ark. Would we at last succeed?

Last Hope Monastery
'They shall take down the covering veil and cover the Ark of the Testimony with it' Numbers 4:5.

Using his zoom, Mathew took a photo of this church standing far off in the distance. We started to hike towards this high destination, crossing through various villages and like fire the news began to spread that foreigners were in the area. Three children came running towards us, with more coming after them. Before long we had a whole army of young people and children, who hoped we would take time out from our mission to throw a football around with them. When we complied with their requests a wave of laughter broke out.

Then with a large crew, we crossed through this area and delved between various routes as the young people argued about the fastest pathway to the top. When we arrived at the gate on the other side of the hill, we found this was not just one church, but a monastery. One of the priests welcomed us in and led us to the storage facility where he brought out a selection of relics, from old crosses, to handwritten and elaborately decorated copies of various books of the Bible.

Most of our entourage were bored and left us to go back to their homes. Then we began to take the last few steps towards the church on the hill, at the highest point of Axum. Leading us inside, the priest showed us some old Christian artwork and there was a small door that led into their holy place, where the Ark rested. We walked over to the Holy of Holies asking if we could enter and see the Ark's replica.

I cannot fully explain why, perhaps it was sheer desperation, but I hoped this priest would allow us through the veil to see the Ark. The church was deficient in size and just a few tantalising steps away the Ark was sitting, but the priest simply said, "No." It felt like we had travelled to the ends of the earth on our quest for the Ark and this

was going to be the end of our endeavour! In a final futile attempt, I walked around the back of the church, where a small opening ten feet above the ground allowed a little light into the Holy of Holies, and I placed our specialised one inch video camera extension into it. The viewer display revealed nothing more than a few flickers of light in a dark room. We then watched the sun go down and walked back down the valley to prepare to leave, and the sad realisation hit us that we would exit this nation without being able to see the Ark's replica. Suddenly something happened that changed everything. Mathew began to talk with a local man who reminded us that Ethiopia has a different calendar to the West and the following day was the beginning of their Easter celebrations, in which a replica of the Ark

of the Covenant would be carried around town! So we cancelled our plans to leave and awoke early the next day to finally see their Ark!

Seeing Ethiopia's Ark

'When you see the Ark of the Covenant...and the Levites bearing it, then you shall set out from your place and go after it' Joshua 3:3.

At four in the morning, we prepared for our long walk from the other side of town where we stayed to the monastery of the Ethiopian Ark. The streets were desolate and we hoped a vehicle would pass by in order to hitch a lift. We began to jog towards the monastery, until someone passed by and picked us up. The streets were still quiet and we wondered if the information we had received was correct. Would a replica of Ethiopia's Ark finally come out from their Holy of Holies? Then as we got closer, we began to see a few pilgrims appear from the side streets, dressed in white from head to toe. We felt a deep sense of relief that finally, after all this time we would get to see a replica of the Ethiopian Ark of the Covenant.

When we arrived outside of the monastery, we felt like strangers in an alien land. We were the only foreigners in a sea of Ethiopians, all dressed in white, holding candles. Then the people began to chant Christian songs. We had never heard anything like it before. It felt like we had stepped back in time to a civilisation that was bypassed by the modern world, where religious pilgrimage was still the central theme of one's life. Then suddenly, the moment we had waited for came as the priests emerged from the monastery carrying a replica of their Ark! Balancing the medium-sized rectangular box above his head, the priest put it on the central altar in town, which came from an ancient church. It was smaller than the Bible's description and it was covered in a dark red material; but we were glad to finally see it!

After about forty-five minutes of prayer and meditation, the chief priest took the Ark off the altar and placed it above his head. The men then began to walk in groups, followed by the women, with the Ark in the middle. As the pilgrimage around town started, a chant began at the front of the procession, leading in waves of sound all the way to the back. This chant always ended with the women and the sound of Ethiopian women singing or speaking is unlike any other we have ever heard. They are softly spoken, almost childlike. The sound is calming, gentle and friendly. We could liken it to a whisper or even a whimper. This was the sound that ended every section of praise to God. Then from the front, the chant would begin once again. We walked around town with the pilgrims and we could not use our camera flash, and our video camera had to be discreet.

We spent two hours in the presence of this Ark and we found a deep respect for the faith of these people. Yet we immediately recognised inconsistencies between the biblical description of the Ark and the Ethiopian Ark. It was the wrong size (Exodus 25:10-11, 37:1), the cherubims and the mercy seat were absent (Exodus 25:17-18); also the four rings on the sides and the poles for carrying it were omitted (Exodus 25:12-13). The greatest problem with the ceremony was the priests carried the Ark contrary to biblical law, which was a sin so grievous that it warranted immediate death (1 Samuel 6:19, 2 Sam. 6:6-9, 1 Chronicles 15:12-13). Another difficulty concerned the thousands of replicas of the Ethiopian Ark which have been made; in the Bible there was only one Temple where the Ark rested. In addition, the Ethiopian timeline is amiss, for the Bible states that the Ark was still in Jerusalem hundreds of years after the Ethiopians claimed to have taken it back to their nation (2 Chronicles 35:3).

Finally, we have the major problem of the theological argument for the use of the Ark of the Covenant within the Church. Now we must accept that theological persuasions do vary in the global Christian Church; in spite of this, there are some central doctrines that unite every believer in Christ Jesus. These doctrines are not to be found by studying the practices of any particular denomination, but can only be anchored in the teachings of the Bible itself. Before any doctrine is re-introduced into the worldwide Church, Christians have to ask themselves: Was this the doctrine of the early apostles? Is this what Paul, Peter and the disciples of the Lord taught? In other words, can we find this teaching in the biblical text and was this the religious observance of the first Christians in the New Testament? The Bible should be the source of all Christian practice, not tradition.

We must therefore start our evaluation of the Ethiopian tradition by considering the teaching of Jeremiah the prophet. Jeremiah was present in Jerusalem when the Babylonians destroyed Solomon's Temple and many years before, he prophesied that the Ark of the Covenant would lose its central role in true worship, and would not be made or visited anymore, Jeremiah 3:16. Within his lifetime, the Ark went missing and his prophecy was being fulfilled.

One of the major theological contentions this Church has is the error of practicing the idea of there being a 'veil' between God and man. The Church is divided, with the Holy of Holies being off-limits to God's people; but when Jesus died the veil in the Second Temple of Jerusalem was torn in two, Matthew 27:51, Mark 15:38, Luke 23:45. This indicates that those who put their faith in Christ's death and resurrection can now enter into the Holiest Place because of Jesus' perfect sacrifice. The Bible says we can 'enter the Presence beyond the veil' Hebrews 6:19. However, the Ethiopian Ark of the Covenant is still hidden and the way into their Holiest Place is still sealed. This contradicts the teaching of Hebrews 9, which confirms that the Ark of the Covenant and the layout of the Tabernacle was symbolic. 'The Holy Spirit indicating that the way into the Holiest of All was not yet manifest' Hebrews 9:8. We therefore learn that the divisions of the Tabernacle and Temple were designed to teach man that his sin has made it impossible for him to enter into God's holy presence, for 'all have sinned and fall short of the glory of God.'

This spiritual division was symbolically witnessed in the Tabernacle and Temple, where God's presence was always off-limits. When the veil in the Temple was torn in two, it bore witness to the fact that those who repent and put their faith in Christ's death and resurrection can have 'boldness to enter the Holiest by the blood of Jesus' Hebrews 10:19-20. The visible veil has been removed.

In the very early days of the Christian Church, the apostles had to discern if those who put their faith in Christ still had to fulfil the rituals of the Old Testament law. After much prayer, debate and testimony of God's blessings to the non-Jews, they agreed that Christians were freed from fulfilling Jewish customs, Acts 15. The law of the Old Testament was kept inside the Ark, but the New Testament reveals this law was a shadow of the good things to come in Christ, Hebrews 10:1. It was not the complete, but the forerunner. Christians should not look back to the Ark, but forward to Christ.

The Ark represented the promise that something better would come and Christ is the fulfilment of that promise. If we now try to put the Ark back into the central place of worship, it will take the emphasis off of Christ and set it onto a special object instead.

The two tablets of the Old Covenant were kept inside the Ark, but Christ's sacrifice created a New Covenant between God and man. The Apostle Paul was the most prolific teacher of the early Church and as an expert in Jewish law he also understood the transforming power of Christ's resurrection. The Ark of the Covenant was a sign of the separation between God and man, and inside the Ark was placed the law that no human was able to keep. The Ark reminded mankind of the impossibility of salvation. Nonetheless, the impossible requirements of the law were satisfied through the death of Christ. Paul wrote the law was our tutor which brought us to Christ, and only Jesus could fulfil and therefore abolish the law, Galatians 2:16, 3:24, Ephesians 2:15. Paul himself preached that those who believe in Christ's death and resurrection can be justified from all things, which could not be forgiven under the law of Moses, Acts 13:39. The impossible was now possible by faith.

Therefore Christians do not need a sacred box, hidden behind a veil, containing law. In Christ there is no veil. The law was fulfilled in Christ and only through faith in Him can we enter into His fulfilment.

> **Legends of the Ark**
> 'But know this, that in the last days perilous times will come; men will be lovers of themselves, lovers of money...' 2 Timothy 3:1-2.

It is true that the Bible locates some Jews in Ethiopia before the time of Christ and in 1983 modern Israel recognised the Jewish presence in the nation by airlifting some of them back to Israel, giving them citizenship. In Ethiopia, we found a deep respect for the sincere faith of the Orthodox Christians, though we had to conclude that their Ark of the Covenant did not meet the biblical requirements to be the original Ark of the Covenant. Therefore, if the Ark is not located in Ethiopia, where is it? Many scholars believe the Ark was destroyed by the Babylonians, for its gold was substantial and the wood was heavy and worthless to them. However, the Hebrews were meticulous bureaucrats keeping lengthy records of treasures lost and taken, yet in all the accounts there is no mention of the sacred Ark, 2 Kings 24:13-14, 2 Kings 25:8-17, 2 Chronicles 36:18-19, Ezra 1:7-10, Jeremiah 52:17-22, Daniel 5:1-3.

Over the centuries, many legends for the location of the Ark have been presented and most people find the wild claims too difficult to distinguish from the plausible. Therefore, we decided to study the other legends of the Ark, to examine the genuine possibilities and more importantly to disregard those which have no credibility.

Legends of the Ark are established on many foundations; some are ancient writings, others are biblical clues and a few are based on myths, dreams and highly charged imaginations. Experts call the latter pseudoarchaeology. This includes archaeological excavations, publications and 'artefacts' which disregard accepted archaeological methodology, do not conform to standard data collecting techniques, and refuse to accept examination, and critiques from professional archaeologists. It is obviously evident that many scholars differ on numerous interpretations of the meaning of artefacts retrieved from antiquity and concerning their dating; yet scholars should agree on the accepted methods of excavations, and data should always be available to those who wish to test any claim or discovery.

For example, in 2003 an artefact appeared in Israel called the Jehoash Inscription, with an ancient Hebrew engraving including the name 'Solomon.' This would have been the first time the name of the Bible's Solomon had been found; however the discovery of this relic was hazy, it lacked authenticated provenance, the owner was secretive and doubts were raised. After a thorough investigation, it was revealed that an intelligent man had forged the inscription and had scammed the experts through tedious research. On the other hand, the Tel Dan Stele, which is inscribed with the 'House of David' was found by an excellent archaeologist, giving us a precise location of the discovery and an exact excavation layer. This signifies that we can trust this antiquity and confirm its date. Knowing the exact location of the discovery is as important as the interpretation of the artefact. With this in mind, pottery is of absolute importance in the dating and excavation of archaeological layers; for its uniformity helps to determine the age of discoveries from antiquity.

As broadcasters and authors, it was expedient for us to be able to distinguish between genuine skilled archaeological discoveries and pseudoarchaeology, which have no credibility. Experts disagree on the meaning of discoveries from antiquity, but they should not disagree on the professionalism of excavations.

In this inquiry, our mission involves broadcasting the artefacts that have been found and evaluating the meaning of them in the light of expert opinion. Clearly we are not involved in the task of excavation, for our job is to examine all the theories, ideas and published work of experts, and to deliver a broad presentation. Only by evaluating the entire body of work can we come to meaningful conclusions. We have to consider every angle, and ask why archaeologists came to their conclusions and why other experts contest them. In this light, we believe we are able to see the larger picture, rather than just one opinion, which may be abstract, distant or contended.

As mentioned in earlier chapters, there are often two ways for people to examine the Bible and archaeological discoveries. The first is to stress what has not been found, the other is to shed light on what has been found. The secular media usually approaches the Bible focusing on what has not been detected and quickly overlooks what has been; this leads to doubt. However, after spending time to study what has been retrieved, we learn that a substantial body of evidence has already been recovered to confirm the accuracy of Scripture. Many theories have disputed the authority of the Bible, yet when new finds vanquished these, they rarely get press. Also, we have many unique biblical finds, but the legends get the publicity!

The Knights Templar
'Even those from afar shall come and build the Temple of the Lord' Zechariah 6:15.

The Templar Knights existed for approximately two centuries during the Middle Ages. They were considered to be the Special Forces of the Crusader period, for their skilled fighting units and expertise. As European Knights their mission was to serve and protect pilgrims to the Holy Land, originally gaining little for themselves. In 1129, they were officially endorsed by the Roman Catholic Church and they helped free the Holy Land from Islamic rule, setting up their base in Jerusalem on the sacred Temple Mount. This order of Knights made pilgrimages safe for Christians to visit the Holy Land and operated a medieval banking fund, allowing a pilgrim to put money into a 'Templar Bank' in London and withdraw it in the Middle East. With the charges on these exchanges and the glory earned for their skills, the Templar Knights became wealthy, and spent their riches building churches around Europe, and Castles in the Middle East. During this period, the Knights Templar had full access to the Temple Mount, where Solomon's Temple once stood. Consequently, some have claimed that this order excavated on the Temple Mount and found the golden treasures of Solomon, including the Ark of the Covenant and smuggled them back into Europe, to hide them all beneath various churches in France, England and Scotland etc.

However, this powerful order, which was once the hero of all Europe, fell out of favour with the King of France and their secret initiation ceremonies led to mistrust and accusations. Many were tortured into confirming charges made against them and in 1312, the Pope dissolved them. The rapid disbanding of the premier European organisation of their age and the transfer of their wealth into other hands, led to the proposal that their treasures were spirited away and hidden in various churches, never to be seen again.

The Temple Church in London was built in the late 12th century by the Knights Templar as their English headquarters. Designed to resemble the Church of the Holy Sepulchre in Jerusalem, it is now famous for the effigy tombs, where Knights lay in wait for the resurrection. This church featured in *The Da Vinci Code*. Rosslyn Chapel in Scotland also appeared in the book and the facts about it remind us that this book is fiction, for the chapel was built a century and a half after the dissolution of the Knights Templar. Historians also confirm that the family who built the chapel testified against the Templar Knights when they were on trial. The crypt of this chapel has been sealed for many years, allowing imaginations to project fantasies that the Holy Grail, the Templar Treasures or the Ark may be in a subterranean vault, below the secret stairway.

Those who search after the treasures of the Knights Templar follow clue after clue, from stained glass windows, architectural mysteries, to ancient images. This quest for the treasure of the Templar Knights has more in common with Hollywood, than history. The Knights Templar continues to inspire imaginations because they are regularly portrayed in books, on TV, films and in computer games. When a rich and powerful organisation suddenly falls and its wealth vanishes, the unanswered questions left behind remain to tantalise subsequent generations. Over the centuries, facts and myth intertwine and legend begins. Nevertheless, in the modern era new investigations propose that the financial problems of the King of France made the dissolution of the Templar Knights a convenient act, which helped solved many of France's problems.

Some have alleged that these Knights found the chambers of the first and second Temples in Jerusalem. However, archaeologists have been able to excavate many of the Templar Knights locations, and are able to give us a proposal of how much they achieved in their search. In Jerusalem itself, many tunnels and chambers have been uncovered, which appear to have been unopened since the time of Christ and if Solomon's treasures had been retrieved, they would have been paraded about, as was the case with many other 'relics' which the Templar's possessed. Yet, the question of the depth of the Temple Mount evacuation remains unanswered.

In the 1930s during British rule in Jerusalem, the director of the British Mandate Antiquities Department carried out the only official archaeological excavation under the Al-Aqsa Mosque, on the Temple Mount. R.W. Hamilton's photo archive of this project shows a Byzantine mosaic floor underneath the mosque, suggesting it was built on the site of a church / monastery. The exact penetration of the Templar Knights on the Temple Mount is open to speculation, but with excavation forbidden, it appears little more will be known until the situation changes. At the present time, the evidence suggests that the only secret treasure that the Templar Knights bereft to this generation is the unending treasure of the imagination.

Parker's Dome of the Rock Excavation
'They have taken treasure and precious things'
Ezekiel 22:25.

I found a copy of several newspaper pages dating back one hundred years ago, whose headlines state: 'Fear Diggers took Ark of the Covenant,' 'Gone with Treasures that was Solomon's' and 'Have Englishmen found the Ark of the Covenant?' Jerusalem was in uproar, rioters were mobbing the streets and the Dome of the Rock was immediately shut. On the run were several members of the 1909-11 Parker Expedition, which had received official permits to excavate in the land, but who in desperation had illegally entered the Dome of the Rock to dig. A century later, I stumbled upon these forgotten reports in my research.

The newspapers read like a movie script, containing reports that Solomon's wealth may have been found and stolen. The leader of the expedition was Captain Montague Parker, who had raised a great deal of money, worth millions today, based on the conviction that Valter H. Juvelius had detected a Bible code in Ezekiel's book. This code could only be understood in ancient Hebrew and to them it revealed the whereabouts of the Temple treasures. The prophet Ezekiel witnessed first hand the fall of Judea to the Babylonians and he lived to become a Babylonian captive, where the Ark may have gone. Based upon new discoveries in Jerusalem and Juvelius' Bible code, a new theory was proposed, and the explorers drew up maps, sketches and clues to assist them, along with archaeological finds.

Just forty years before, British archaeologist Charles Warren had found a complex of tunnels in the Holy Land and with Jerusalem's unknown tunnels being rediscovered the Parker Expedition believed they could uncover the lost Jewish treasure. In 1909, they arrived in Jerusalem with a permit, but were not allowed on the Mount itself.

They began to excavate by the Gihon Spring, six hundred metres to the south of the Mount, laboriously clearing Hezekiah's Tunnel and other labyrinths. The Parker team found themselves in the tunnel that the Bible's King Hezekiah had ordered to be made, before 701BC. 'It was Hezekiah who blocked the upper outlet of the Gihon Spring and channelled the water down to the west side of the City of David' 2 Chronicles 32:30. 'As for the other events of

Hezekiah's reign, all his achievements and how he made the pool and the tunnel by which he brought water into the city...' 2 Kings 20:20. This tunnel is another proof of the Bible's accuracy in its description of ancient history.

Controversy soon arose that not one member of the team was a professional archaeologist and it was alleged they had inexhaustible funds in order to bribe the locals. As the years passed, they penetrated labyrinths underground, but they were still too far away from the Temple Mount. Pressure mounted on the team, as the financial backers began to demand results, just at the same time the permit to excavate from the Turks was ending. What would they do?

In a desperate attempt, Parker's team bribed the locals, wore Arab clothes and secretly entered the Temple Mount digging in the southeast corner of Solomon's Stables. Still with no success, on the fateful night of 17 April 1911, the excavators entered the Dome of the Rock, having made a deal with the Muslim in charge and began lowering themselves into the cavern inside. Reports later suggested the men had smashed through rock to find a shaft below, but their noise was heard and a Muslim attendant cried out to raise an alarm. The team quickly fled, fearing for their lives at worst, their freedom at best. In the chaos of the next few days, rumours spread that the Ark of the Covenant, Solomon's Crown and other precious artefacts had been stolen. In fact, Parker and his team escaped out of the region empty handed on a boat, never to return.

One hundred years later these press reports still inspire an Indiana Jones moment, but in truth, they are a perfect example of how secrecy, misinformation, speculation and the media's desire to get attention can create myth. The Parker Expedition had sought relics for profit; it ended with a quick exit, no artefacts and the investors losing their money. Nevertheless, the drawings of the excavation of the tunnel still serve us and visitors to Israel can enter this tunnel oblivious to the reason why it was excavated in secrecy.

> **Mount Nebo and Jeremiah**
> 'Now Jeremiah remained in the court of the prison until the day that Jerusalem was taken'
> Jeremiah 38:28.

Mount Nebo, located in western Jordon, is 2,680 feet above sea level and on a clear day Jerusalem can be seen from the top. It was on this mountain that the Bible states Moses went to view the Promised Land, Deuteronomy 34:1. Mount Nebo is also famed as the resting place for the Ark of the Covenant. The apocryphal book of 2 Maccabees 2:4-7, claims the following account of Jeremiah: 'The prophet being warned of God, commanded the Tabernacle and the Ark to accompany him, as he went forth into the mountain, where Moses climbed up (Mount Nebo) and saw the inheritance of God.' He 'found a hollow cave, wherein he laid the Tabernacle and the Ark and the altar of incense, and so stopped the door. Then some of those that followed him came up to mark the place, but they could not find it.' The book then suggests that Jeremiah was angry with these people for trying to record the location and told them, "The place shall be unknown until the time that God gathers His people again together and receives them unto mercy."

The book itself dates to around 190BC and may have been written by rebel Jews in Alexandria, Egypt. It surfaced many centuries after the time of Jeremiah and was rejected by the Jews as non-historical, and not inspired by God. Protestants follow in the tradition of the Jews, stating the book is neither historical, nor inspired and state its contents contradict the teaching of Scripture. The apostles in their letters never quoted from it. Scholars believe the first book of Maccabees contains some historical value, but the second is mostly fiction, with little to offer. This imaginary story of Jeremiah hiding the Ark and other items is also out of sync with history, for the prophecy stated these objects would have been found and returned to God's people when the Lord gathered, 'His people again together,' which happened when the ancient Jews returned from Babylon.

Nonetheless, these facts have not dissuaded people to hunt for the Ark on this mountain and in 1981 an American explorer claimed to have found the Ark in Mount Nebo; he even took an illusive photo which I was able to track down. The length of this 'Ark' is 62 inches long, and its height and width are both 37 inches. A strip of wood went around the edges of the Ark, with one in the centre dividing the main wooden panels in half. The pattern on the lining appeared as tiny flowers and the two divided panels at the front were engraved with a criss-cross pattern. This box was covered in brass, not gold. One archaeologist who studied this case established that the photo proved undeniably that this Ark was made with modern materials, which can only be sourced today. This claim sunk as fast as it had arisen and even conspiracy hunters are relatively calm about it. The story of this find was exciting to read, nevertheless it is interesting to note that many 'finds' of the Ark all came about at the same time as Hollywood's Indiana Jones retrieved it! Like many other accounts of people finding the Ark, this man also made claims to Noah's Ark, the Tower of Babel and others. His discovery was also aligned to a prophecy that he gave in the 1980s, in which he would become one of the 144,000 described in the outline of the end times in Revelation 14:1, and that the return of Christ would take place in the 1980s. He never explained why he didn't find any of the other biblical articles that were also 'hidden by Jeremiah.'

With the excitement of the discovery of the Dead Sea Scrolls, numerous caves in this region have been excavated, but there is no sign of the Ark. It is also important to remember that Jeremiah was considered as an enemy of the Levites because of his prophecies of the fall of Judah. The Levites were the only people who had access to the Ark and they would not have allowed him to take it away. Secondly, it would be impossible for Jeremiah to have been able to hide the Ark before the Babylonians came, for the Bible states that he was in prison, Jeremiah 37-39. This falsified story of 'Jeremiah' is not historical, it is not inspired and its claims contradict Scripture.

The Garden Tomb Controversy
'Test everything; hold fast what is good'
1 Thessalonians 5:21.

The most scandalous report of the discovery of the Ark was made by an amateur archaeologist who had excavated in Zedekiah's Cave and at the Garden Tomb in Jerusalem; claiming to have detected the blood of Christ on the mercy seat of the Ark, below where Jesus may have been crucified. This explorer was in Jerusalem when he alleged his arm involuntarily pointed to a destination and out of his mouth came words over which he had no control, "That's Jeremiah's Grotto and the Ark of the Covenant is buried in there." This same individual claimed to have found Noah's Ark and other artefacts and places. However, we identified many Christian scholars who trust the Bible, as well as archaeologists, historians, scientists and even members of his team that argue these claims have no validity.

Therefore we had to investigate this claim to learn if it had any substance. Our starting point was to evaluate the eyewitness accounts of those who were present during the excavation. The two sons of the explorer were filmed in Israel in 2007, eight years after their father's death. Outside of Zedekiah's Cave one said, "My dad believed there are some tunnel systems under Jerusalem that take you all the way to the skull mountain, where Christ was crucified." They alleged that a secret iron door was detected in a tunnel from Zedekiah's Cave and one said, "I was here in 2005 with the group and we searched for the iron door…and we never found the door again." The two sons obviously had a respect for their father and they believed in his stories. Their dad alleged that many people had tried to find the same tunnel, and they had been struck dead, but no bodies were ever found. "That's why my dad was very secretive about" the location of the Ark "even to people he knew and trusted."

This theory has been widely publicised among Christian groups, therefore the Israeli Antiquities Authority and the Christians who run the Garden Tomb believed this claim warranted a professional excavation. They also asked for the assistance of the late explorers Archaeological Foundation to show the way. After the inquiry, the two sons stated that the investigators "did underground radar scans, looking for tunnel systems and they've dug a good way in and so far they haven't really found anything of a tunnel system...nobody has found that tunnel." Then outside of the Garden Tomb, which is close to Zedekiah's Cave, one of the sons pointed to a hole in the ground where they entered saying, "We went downward. At first there was a lot of loose rock, but then we had to start using jack hammers and chisels, and it was very hard work going down. Even the drill bits, some of the best you can buy, couldn't penetrate" it. Speaking of the professional team he said, "They haven't found the chamber where the Ark of the Covenant rests. My dad said that when he saw the Ark of the Covenant the whole room was glowing...he never told us actually where it was because he was afraid."

A letter dated 8 August 1996, was sent by Joe Zias, then Curator of Anthropology / Archaeology of the Israeli Antiquities Authority. It stated that this explorer 'is neither an archaeologist nor has he ever carried out a legally licensed excavation in Israel or Jerusalem. In order to excavate one must have at least a BA in archaeology...We are aware of his claims...they have no scientific basis whatsoever, nor have they ever been published in a professional journal.' As these alleged finds became more famous, more doubts arose over them. As a result some Australian Christians sent a letter to the Israeli Antiquities Authority asking if these theories were legitimate. The response dated 16 November 1998 was shown to the explorer. It states: 'We cannot confirm these finds and have no information about them.' The explorer 'has never received a license from the Israeli Antiquities Authority to excavate in Israel. If he says he has excavated in Israel, he has committed an illegal act, since every excavation in Israel must be licensed by our authority...legitimate archaeological finds are published in professional journals or by universities and other recognised scientific institutes' - Osnat Goaz, spokeswoman for the Department of Education Information.

The amateur archaeologist was a Seventh Day Adventist and as a prominent member, the denomination investigated his 'finds' and dismissed them. Another Seventh Day Adventist believed the claims needed a thorough assessing and published a book with direct conclusions. The Rev. R. Fisher reviewed the book stating that it was 'a meticulously, painstakingly' examination of the alleged finds. 'They were just claims - the product of a fertile imagination. There was no testable evidence put forth.' No archaeological permits were ever produced and the account of what was seen 'at the Garden Tomb site differs greatly from all the co-workers and eyewitnesses.'

We then decided we must examine the final reports of the professional excavations. In the 2006 report by the Garden Tomb (Jerusalem) Association, to the UK Charity Commission, we identified that the Trustees had authorised the Israeli Antiquities Authority, with the assistance of the late explorer's Archaeological Foundation 'to carry out an excavation, in the hope of discovering artefacts dating back to biblical times. As it happens nothing of any historical interest or value was unearthed.' This was the first time that the late explorer's foundation had been present at an official excavation and nothing to substantiate these claims was found.

In the report on the Garden Tomb excavation, the Israeli Antiquities Authority in Journal 118, dated 20 March 2006, with permit No. A-4549, stated that 'during the 1980s' this explorer had 'excavated several underground chambers at the site. The current excavation cleaned and documented the former chambers and additional chambers were excavated.' This professional team was therefore able to find the chambers that had been entered by the amateur archaeologist, but only a few finds of glass and other basic objects were retrieved stating: 'The finds were disturbed by the previous excavation.' In 2010, Journal 122 of the Israeli Antiquities Authority contained the final report of the 2007 excavation, permit No. A-5222, and it added very little to their previous conclusion. The excavations at Zedekiah's Cave in addition proved that no shred of evidence has ever been found to substantiate any of the alleged discoveries. Finally, Hebrews 9:11, 22-24, states that Christ's blood purified in the perfect tabernacle in heaven, not on earthly copies.

The Lemba Jews of South Africa
'Arise, O Lord, to Your resting place, You and the Ark of your strength' Psalm 132:8.

In Southern Africa an overlooked ethnic group of tens of thousands of people made an astonishing claim. They believed they were descendants of the Jews of the Bible! When scholars first arrived to study them, it was impossible to distinguish them physically from the African tribes around them, yet they found many religious practices similar to Judaism. They believe in one God called Nwali, they have a holy day like the Sabbath, they do not eat certain foods and they practice circumcision. Did missionaries accidentally introduce these observances or does this legacy go back further? According to oral tradition their ancestors were Jews and genetic testing in 1996 identified that fifty percent of the Lemba Y chromosomes were Semitic in origin, and later studies confirmed their genetic heritage.

Lemba tradition spoke of a drum-like object, the 'Ngoma Lungundu' which was carried by poles and one professor alleged this was the Ark, tracing the Lemba's possible journey from Judea to Yemen, across the Red Sea into Africa. The remains of this wooden drum were found and at 45 inches long, 24 wide and 27 tall, it looks like a giant half-broken shell of a walnut. Many scholars seem bewildered how an African drum, which has been carbon dated to just over 600 years ago is now being linked to the Ark. Some scholars suggest that the mistake made was to project the Bible's concept of the Ark onto African culture, where the traditions of sacred and powerful drums have long existed. Some Africans were also angry that an original African artefact was being claimed to be of foreign origin.

The Bible dates the original Ark to over three millennia ago and a copy should at least have some physical similarity to it. This drum was found discarded in a cave in the 1940s by missionaries, who took it to a Zimbabwean museum and it was later lost in conflict. It was then found and forgotten again in a museum's back room. Now this claim has plucked it from obscurity and its status has been raised in this museum. The suggestion that a core of the original Ark may be detected inside this drum has no standing and experts have stated that African drums should be respected for being just that. However, international press reports should help get more tourists into this African museum, even if the display of the 'Ark' disappoints.

The Copper Scroll Treasure Hunt
'He drove them all out of the Temple...and poured out the changers' money and overturned the tables' John 2:15.

In 1947, a young shepherd boy threw a stone into a cave and heard the sound of shattering pottery. Entering he discovered the Dead Sea Scrolls, the greatest, finest and oldest complete source of biblical text ever found. One expert said, "We've got every book of the Hebrew Bible there, except Esther." Two millennia ago, "They were reading and writing and believing what we are today, with almost no details lost in the transition over two thousand years!" Dating from around the time of Christ, these 900 texts were found in over 15,000 pieces in eleven caves. These biblical texts prove we still have the same Hebrew Bible that the first century Jews used! Other texts were also found which describe the beliefs of the Essenes Jewish sect, who copied and made the texts in the region.

In 1952, in cave three on the shores of the Dead Sea, a metal scroll was found and after analysis it proved to be 99.9% copper, which was a valuable material. The information on the scroll must have been very exceptional for the cost of the copper suggested they could not risk losing the contents. With great care, experts cut the scroll into many tiny pieces and found inscribed the locations for sixty-four treasures buried in the Holy Land! 'In the outer valley, in the middle of the circle on the stone, buried at seventeen cubits beneath it; 17 talents of gold and silver!'

Why was this treasure list guarded by a secret community of Jews, whose writings suggest they had rejected worldly wealth and embraced poverty? Scholars have often debated over its meaning. Could it list King Solomon's wealth? Probably not, because it dates to the time of the Second Temple and it describes tithe money that appears to be from the Second Temple period. 'In the mouth of the spring of the Temple, vessels of silver and gold for tithe and money; the whole being six hundred talents.' Does this list describe what happened to the tithe from the Temple that Rome destroyed?

Some have suggested the Copper Scroll may have been a hoax. Was this list the last laugh of a people who despised riches? Other scholars think it could be a coded map; as an example, 'Go to London Bridge, hidden inside the well beside, thirty pieces of silver,' but the code really means, 'Go to Westminster Bridge...' This idea flourished from the text stating: 'In a dry well at Kohlt...a copy of this document with its explanation...and an inventory.'

Guided by these texts, many adventurers have raised millions of dollars to go on a treasure hunt, chasing clues dating back two millennia. In 1992, one American claimed he found holy anointing oil and incense, others are still digging. One report on an American News programme featured another explorer calling him an 'amateur treasure hunter.' He said, "I've broken the code on the Copper Scroll!...I'm going to guess it's three billion worth of gold and silver alone...There are bags of gems." Many years have passed and the team have still detected nothing. On one dig, the Israeli Antiquities Authority refused the team permission to dig where they wanted. Professional archaeologists have actually made major concessions to allow amateurs to search in Israel, because if a dig disturbs a relic which was buried two millennia ago, we only have one chance to document accurately the how, when and where of its discovery. If mistakes are made, we cannot go back asking for a second chance. Archaeological investigations are supposed to be painstaking tasks.

In 1998, the BBC interviewed one American who claimed he was close to finding the Ark of the Covenant. Joe Zias from Israel's Antiquity Authority told the BBC, "He has no academic qualifications whatsoever - he's more of an adventurer." Many of these explorers believe the scroll identifies items from the First Temple, yet the text also contains Greek letters and Alexander the Great only conquered the land in 332BC. The Copper Scroll is not a map to the lost Ark.

Those who follow clues from the Copper Scroll often seem sincere, but no proof has been found which satisfies or verifies the scholarly desire for evidence. Their discoveries are perpetually very close and always just a few feet away. The only current exception to the many eccentric adventurers is an archaeologist of the Hebrew University of Jerusalem, who is excavating legitimately using the Copper Scroll as his guide. At the moment he has identified a long tunnel in the Judean wilderness, filled with a great deal of rubble! No treasures listed in the scroll have ever been detected and it could be the case that if it was genuine, the Romans forced the Jews to retrieve it.

Jerusalem's Secret Temple Chamber
'I will give you the treasures of darkness and hidden riches of secret places' Isaiah 45:3.

The Bible meticulously records the fate of the Temple treasures, yet it never details the loss of the Ark. Why is this? When this question is put to leading Rabbis they often smile and declare, "The lost Ark of the Covenant was never lost at all!" According to this Jewish legend, a secret chamber was made under Solomon's Temple and it was this chamber that kept the Ark safe from Pharaoh Shishak, and all the other invasions of Jerusalem. Some date the chamber to the time of Solomon, others to Josiah. This theory suggests the Levites in accordance with emergency protocol, placed the Ark into the sealed chamber when the Babylonians invaded and it was never retrieved because the Jews were never truly independent, until now.

The Wailing Wall in Jerusalem is the holiest place for Jews. Thirty years ago, two leading Rabbis who were responsible for the Wall, became so convinced of the secret chamber account, that they began an illegal excavation under the Temple Mount to find it and the original Ark within! After many months of digging, they claimed to have broken through into an unknown tunnel, which was sealed for thousands of years. However, after eighteen months of digging and clearing, their secret excavation was discovered and the Israeli authorities under great pressure stopped the dig, and the Muslim authority on the Temple Mount protested until it was sealed. The Ark which felt so near was still out of reach.

There have been many claims to have located a 'secret resting place for the Ark,' yet this account is the only one situated below the site of the two Jewish Temples. It is held by the ancestors of those who served in the Temple and has been propagated by the most senior Rabbis in Israel. These excavators were not discredited adventurers, but revered spiritual leaders and the descendants of the keepers of the Ark. In addition, archaeologists have proved that the Temple Mount contains many tunnels, which are now illegal to excavate. With these facts, it is possible for many to take a leap of faith to suggest one of these may lead to a secret chamber. Testing this theory however, may not only lead to the Ark, but also to attempts to destroy the Dome of the Rock, the beginnings of the building of a new Jewish Temple and a Third World War!

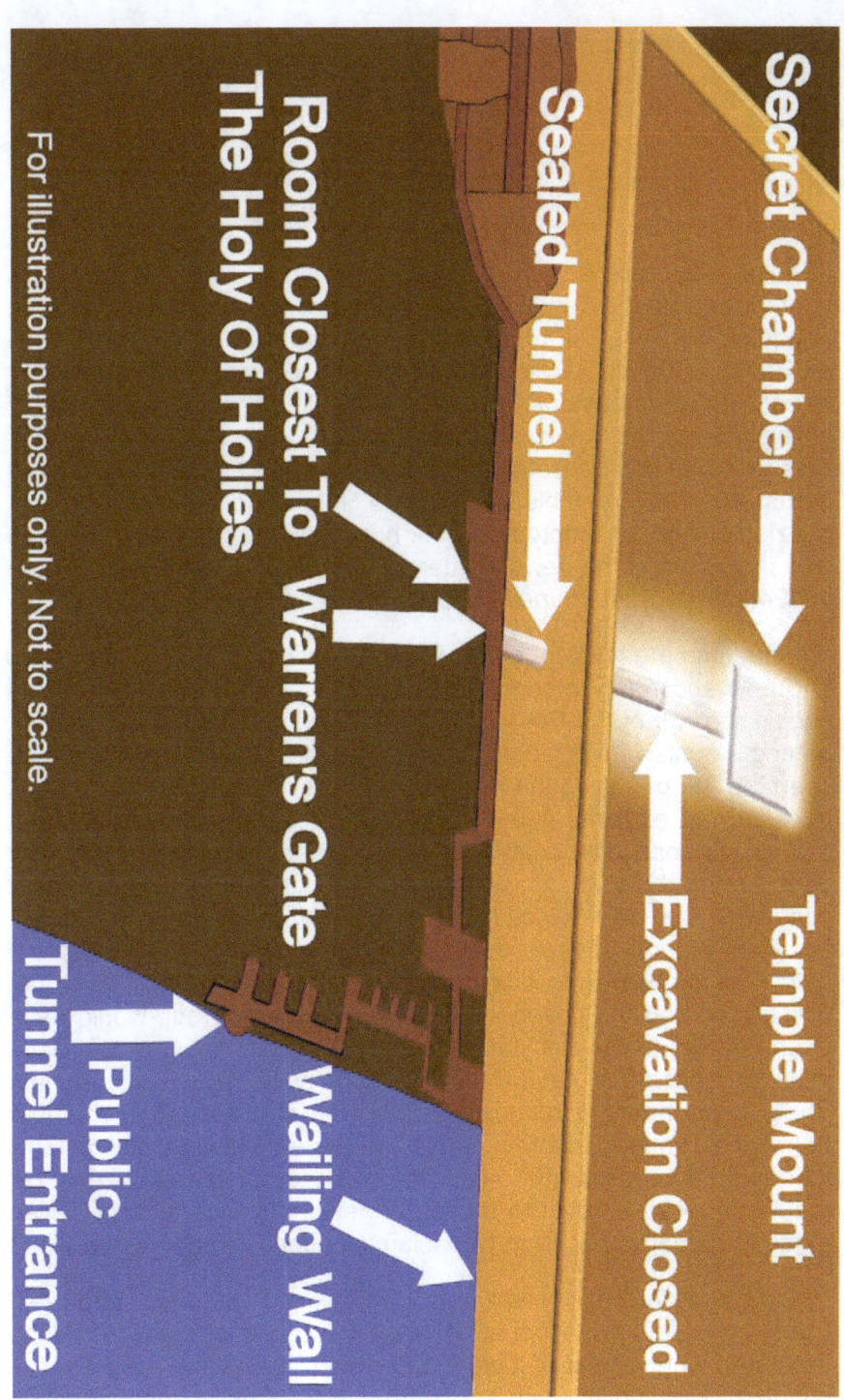

> ## St. John's Revelation of the Heavenly Ark
> 'The Temple of God was opened in heaven and the Ark of His Covenant was seen in His Temple'
> Revelation 11:19.

Those who believe the Ark of the Covenant is locked inside a chamber under the Temple Mount state that it was never retrieved in antiquity, because the dominating threat from foreign powers such as Babylon, Persia, Greece and Rome never ceased. The memory of each invasion became so severe in the Jewish psyche that fear of losing the sacred Ark guaranteed its seclusion under the Temple. This fear was compensated in 63BC, as Rome's Pompey conquered Jerusalem and forced his way into the Holy of Holies. Inside he was puzzled to find an empty space. A hundred years later, the Temple was in ruins and the Jews scattered. Over 1,800 years passed and in 1948, Israel's rebirth gave hope that the Ark could be retrieved.

In that time the mystery of the Ark has captured many imaginations and now according to some leading Rabbis, the true hinderance to finding the Ark of the Covenant is not knowing where to search, but getting permission to search. Many people have alleged to have seen the Ark or solved the mystery, and in our investigation we have travelled far, explored many lands and studied these claims. Some stories fall apart after a little research; others take time to dig very deep to find the truth. Now at the end of our investigation we have concluded that only two cases for the Ark still stand. The first is that the Babylonians destroyed the Ark, burning the wood to get the gold. The problem with this theory is that the two tablets of stone, which recorded the covenant between God and Israel, would have been useless to the Babylonians, and the ancient Jews would have risked everything to save them for posterity. This never happened. The second theory is that the Ark now rests inside a secret chamber below the Temple Mount in Jerusalem, Israel. The problem with this theory is its impossibility to test, for any attempt to excavate below the Mount always leads to unrest, protests, violence and may even trigger a global war starting with Islamic nations invading Israel.

In the hunt for the ancient treasures of the Bible, the sacred text gives us a detailed account of what was once possessed by the Jews and where most of it went. Enormous amounts of wealth were spent on building the Jewish Temples and making the relics that went into them. These items were in turn plundered by Egypt, Syria, Assyria, Arabia, Babylon, Sidon, Tyre, Philistia, Greece and Rome. The monuments of Egypt and Rome prove this loss, as well as the chronicle of the historian Josephus. Yet in the end, the Bible itself indicates that the treasures of the ancient Jews were fleeting.

In the first century, the Jews were still hoping that a Messiah would come and deliver their nation, so they could worship freely. When Christ began to teach, His chief concern was for the souls of men, rather than establishing a wealthy Jewish Kingdom with fleeting riches and temporary treasures. When the disciples stood amazed at the Temple, He prophesied its destruction. To a rich young ruler He said, "Give all to the poor and come follow Me!" In the Temple Jesus overturned the tables of money changers and used a whip to clear it of those who sought profit instead of prayer. Finally His sermons asked penetrating questions concerning the fragility of the soul. In one parable he spoke of a rich man who stored up wealth to live a life of pleasure when God said, "You fool! This very night your soul will be required of you." Jesus challenged those who came to Him and spoke of eternity, hell and the judgment to come asking, "What will a man give in exchange for his soul?"

Treasure hunters still seek the Ark of the Covenant and many claims have been made and continue to be made. Perhaps Jeremiah's prophecy of 3:16 was the final word on the Ark; or maybe John 3:16 was the final word for those who hope to see the Ark once again. The Bible states: 'For God so loved the world that He gave His only begotten Son, that whoever believes in Him should not perish, but have everlasting life.' This time, the precious gift from God was not the design of a golden box, but His only Son. The Apostle John witnessed the life of Christ and in the last days of his life, he saw a vision of Christ in heaven and of the Ark. The Bible itself reveals that eternal life is not a right to be demanded, but a gift to be received by faith. The apostles preached that all need to repent, and put their faith in the death and resurrection of the Lord Jesus Christ, Acts 2:31-40, 13:28-39, Romans 10:8-13. Those who repent and believe the gospel will by faith receive all the mercy obtained by the sacrifice of Jesus on the cross. In addition, the book of Revelation indicates that those who put their faith in Christ may one day get to see the heavenly Ark, in the eternal bliss of their spiritual home. 'God will wipe away every tear from their eyes, there shall be no more death, nor sorrow, nor crying. There shall be no more pain, for the former things have passed away' Revelation 21:4.

ByFaith - Quest for the Ark of the Covenant

If you enjoyed this search for the Ark of the Covenant, you can also watch this investigation on your TV! *ByFaith - Quest for the Ark of the Covenant* DVD contains four episodes.

Episode 1: Tutankhamun's Treasure and the Ark of the Covenant.

Episode 2: Pharaoh Shishak and the Gold of Solomon's Temple.

Episode 3: Jerusalem's Wealth and the Lost Jewish Temple.

Episode 4: A Forgotten Civilisation and the Ark's Legacy.

You can also join Paul and Mathew on their investigation to find the evidence for the Bible's exodus. The *Israel in Egypt / Exodus Mystery* DVD and *The Exodus Evidence* book are now available. Find out more at www.ByFaith.org

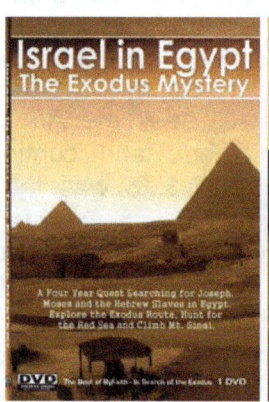

ByFaith - World Mission DVD. Join the brothers Paul and Mathew, as their mission expeditions take them into 14 nations. 85 minutes.

Great Christian Revivals on 1 DVD is an uplifting account of some of the greatest revivals in Church history. Filmed on location across Britain and drawing upon archive information, the stories of the Welsh Revival (1904-1905), the Hebridean Revival (1949-1952) and the Evangelical Revival (1739-1791) are told in this 72-minute documentary.

Visit **www.ByFaith.org** for trailers

ByFaith Media Books

Heaven – A Journey to Paradise by Paul Backholer.

Holy Spirit Power by Paul Backholer.

Samuel Rees Howells: A Life of Intercession by Richard Maton.

Samuel, Son and Successor of Rees Howells by Richard Maton.

How Christianity Made the Modern World by Paul Backholer.

Revival Fires and Awakenings by Mathew Backholer.

Short-Term Missions, A Christian Guide by Mathew Backholer.

Discipleship For Everyday Living by Mathew Backholer.

Global Revival, Worldwide Outpourings by Mathew Backholer.

Understanding Revival by Mathew Backholer.

Revival Fire – 150 Years of Revivals by Mathew Backholer.

Revival Answers: True and False Revivals by Mathew Backholer.

Extreme Faith – On Fire Christianity by Mathew Backholer.

How to Plan, Prepare and Successfully Complete Your Short-Term Mission by Mathew Backholer.

Britain, a Christian Nation by Paul Backholer.

The Holy Spirit in a Man by R.B. Watchman. An autobiography.

Tares and Weeds in your Church by R.B. Watchman.

Prophecy Now, Prophetic Words and Divine Revelations, For You, the Church and the Nations by Michael Backholer.

www.ByFaithBooks.co.uk – www.ByFaithDVDs.co.uk

www.ingramcontent.com/pod-product-compliance
Lightning Source LLC
LaVergne TN
LVHW021717080426
835510LV00010B/1007

9 781788 220019